*To my children Chandra and Danny
who have walked with me through many storms
and survived . . . I love you bunches!*

SURVIVING THE BAD HAIR DAYS

STORIES OF INSPIRATION & HOPE

CHERIE JOBE

© 2014 by Cherie Jobe,
St. Clair Publications

All rights reserved. No part of this publication may be reproduced or transmitted in any form by any means electronic or mechanical, including telecopy, recording, or any information storage and retrieval system now known or invented, without permission in writing from the publisher, except by a reviewer who wishes to quote brief passages in connection with a review written for inclusion in a magazine, newspaper or broadcast.

ISBN 978-1-935786-81-8
Printed in the United States of America

St. Clair Publications
P. O. Box 726
Mc Minnville, TN 37111-0726
http://stclairpublications.com

Cover and Interior Design
Brecca Theele, Theele Design

TABLE OF CONTENTS

Acknowledgments.............................. ix

A Note from a Survivor xi

Foreword..................................... xiii

Introduction: Surviving the Storms of Life xv

Surviving the Big One!................................1

Surviving the Enemy's Plan 7

Surviving the Loss of All My Family.....................11

Surviving Childhood Abuse 23

Surviving a Cheating Spouse.............................29

Surviving Mental Illness..................................35

Surviving the Loss of Two Children....................39

Surviving a Brain Hemorrhage.........................49

Surviving Anorexia and Bulimia.......................57

Surviving a Near-fatal Wreck...........................61

Surviving a Tornado......................................71

Surviving Cancer..77

Surviving a Change in Parenting Plans..................85

Surviving Abuse and Abortion.........................93

Surviving Caregiving....................................101

Surviving Putting Career First........................109

Surviving Chronic Pain................................117

Surviving Waiting for Mr. Right......................125

Surviving Divorce.......................................131

Surviving the Nightmare Boss........................137

Surviving Co-dependency.............................143

Surviving the Loss of Children.......................147

TABLE OF CONTENTS

Surviving Powerlessness..............................151

Looking for Answers While in the Storm? 155

God's Survival Tips 157

    About the Author 167

    Other Books by Cherie Jobe 169

ACKNOWLEDGMENTS

This book was birthed straight from the heart. I am indebted to all those who have believed in, labored with and prayed with me over this book.

My heartfelt gratitude goes to:

My Survivors: Thanks so much for allowing these readers to share your lives—the good, bad, and ugly hair days.

My Best Friend, Companion, Lover and Confidante: Jim Jobe—You have consistently strengthened my life with your love and wise counsel. I am forever thankful for you.

My Ministry Advisory Team: Karen Thrasher, Debbie Garvin, Patsy Highland, Tambra Combs, and Sherri Rambo—

You gals are such a blessing. Without your encouragement and listening ears whenever I have my meltdowns, this book never would have been written. I am honored to call you my sisters in Christ.

My Editor: Cindy Phiffer—Your gift of careful editorial work is outstanding, and your friendship is genuine and loyal.

My Publisher: Stan St. Clair—I am forever grateful for your patience and desire to give God your best.

My Book Designer: Brecca Theele—Thank you for listening to my thoughts and then designing another fabulous cover.

My Savior, Jesus Christ: I thank you for bringing into my life the people, the resources, and the opportunity to complete this work. I offer it to You for Your glory.

A NOTE FROM A SURVIVOR

For 40 years in the beauty industry, I have prided myself on trust, loyalty, and honesty. I value the trust each survivor in this book has given me, so I feel the need to tell you that I have been given permission to share their survival stories with you.

In some situations, their names have been changed to protect their personal identity.

I want to thank each person who has bravely shared his or her personal story. Together, we give Him all the glory, because without Him, there is no hope of survival.

In His army,

Cherie

FOREWORD

Whether it's wisdom while you weave, counsel during the cut, pumped you up during the process, hallelujahs with the highlights, listening during the low lights, or praying during the perm, Cherie is the real deal.

Genuine godly goodness comes from behind her chair, and all the while, she is making you beautiful, inside and out!

Her words on the page are as sincere and restorative as the look in the mirror after she's done her magic.

After you've spent time with Cherie in person or on paper, you will feel valued, worthy, and beautiful. You'll be encouraged and inspired. You'll have renewed promise in your heart. While reading you can almost hear her say, "Come sit down. Let's get you shaped up and positive about yourself. Did you know that God didn't make no junk? You are a queen, girl! We serve a BIG God! Let me show you what HE can do!"

—KIM BOLTON
Author, Speaker, Psalmist
www.KimBolton.com

INTRODUCTION: SURVIVING THE STORMS OF LIFE

Plan. Prepare. Survive.

Being a hairdresser for 40 years, I have learned a few tricks for surviving the Bad Hair Days of Life.

What would you say is the secret ingredient of tough people? Why do they survive the rough times when others are overcome by them? The answer is the Survival Kit they are using.

When it comes to emergency preparedness, it's easy to get lulled into a sense of complacency. It's difficult to face the reality that disaster could strike close to home, even though we've witnessed the devastation that comes from disasters such as Hurricane Katrina, the Asian Tsunami, the tornado that flattened a Kansas town, and the terrorist attacks on 9-11.

A Survival Kit is not something you put together when an emergency happens. It is a bag already filled with lifesaving gear, sitting around waiting for you to pick it up.

When I think about life's problems, I think about Job in the Old Testament. Job lost everything. And it wasn't because God was punishing Job; God was testing him. Just as Job was tried, you and I will be tested too. He lost everything, yet he wasn't a loser because he never turned his back on God.

The key Survival Tip to remember is that no matter what happens on those Bad Hair Days of Life, keep your trust in God and you, too, will be a survivor.

Woven throughout this book is hope. Many of the stories you are about to read are about tough times, but even through tough times, you will hear about how they used their Survival Kit. God's written word is anchored in hope.

Cherie Jobe

SURVIVING THE BIG ONE!

"For I know the plans I have for you," declares the Lord
"plans to prosper you and not to harm you,
plans to give you hope and a future."

JEREMIAH 29:11

It's another beautiful day in paradise, I thought as I scrambled my daily dose of protein. I felt so excited as I put on my makeup and fixed my hair before heading to the salon. Today, I was doing something I rarely got to do. I was celebrating my birthday one day early.

Thankfully, when I arrived at the salon, I checked my appointment book, and it looked like a pretty full day. Clients were coming and going. As usual, I had one under the dryer, one in the chair, and one waiting. Hairstylists are known for our juggling abilities!

Around 10:00, I thought that the eggs didn't settle right with my stomach. By noon, I stirred around the shop trying to get rid of the indigestion before meeting a friend for lunch. On the way to the restaurant, I stopped at the drugstore, got some Mylanta, and turned up the bottle.

People were starting to gather at the Mexican restaurant, but I immediately eyed my friend sitting in the booth eating chips and salsa. By this time, I wasn't feeling well at all. Wouldn't you know it? My favorite food and my only lunch date of the year, and I couldn't eat a thing.

I told my friend that I was puzzled, since I never had indigestion, so I sipped on a Sprite while we talked. She worked for a local doctor and was concerned about me, but I thought it was just a little bump in the road that I needed to push through. I finished my drink in time to make it back to the salon for my 1:00 appointments. Katherine was waiting on me when I got back, and Peggy would be showing up soon.

Around 2:00, I began to notice that I had a toothache. *That's just perfect!* I thought. *I have one client in the chair and one under the dryer. Of all times to have a toothache.*

By this point, my co-workers had overheard me talking about how I was feeling. The lady who worked in the station behind me came over and whispered in my ear, "You do know that women often have jaw pain when they're having a heart attack."

SURVIVING THE BIG ONE

"No way," I said. I had just had some tests run on my heart, and everything was fine.

By 2:30, everything was *not* fine.

I told the lady in the chair that I needed to go to the back room and that I'd be right back. Boy, was I ever wrong!

The moment I sat down, I started sweating, vomiting, and totally losing control of my bodily functions. All I could say was, "Call 9-1-1 and my husband."

Luckily, the ambulance was only about three miles down the road, so they were there pronto!

They put me on a stretcher, strapped me down, and headed to the ER. Like any veteran hairdresser would do, I raised my head on our way out the door and said, "Somebody please take care of my perm—under the dryer."

Hospital staff was waiting on me, ready to stabilize my declining situation. I still wasn't fully understanding what was going on, but I knew one thing for sure: I wasn't in control of a thing. Control was one of the things I had always prided myself in. Having a very painful, dysfunctional childhood resulted in never trusting anyone else with my life.

The doctors came in and said they were sending me to St. Thomas Hospital in Nashville. Their reputation for being the #1 heart institute in the area just made me realize how serious my situation was. My ex-husband had open-heart surgery there, so I was familiar with the doctors. But *I* wasn't supposed to be the one in the bed.

What had begun as a beautiful day had become a living nightmare.

A team of cardiologists met me at the ER, ready to relieve my pain. They rushed me to the cath lab where they did an arteriogram that showed a 100-percent blockage in my main artery.

I woke up in my newly redecorated CCU room surrounded by doctors and family. I could tell by the tears on my family's faces that the news wasn't good.

Dr. Ball explained, "Cherie, you have a major blockage, and we need to fix it now."

"Can't I come back later?" I wondered aloud. This was certainly not in my plans for the day.

"I wouldn't take that chance if I were you," he responded firmly.

No! I thought. *This can't be happening to me.* But sometimes we have to release control and trust those who are in charge and are wiser than we are.

Once the decision had been made to move forward, my family decided to stay at the hotel connected to the hospital. Meanwhile, my heart cried out to the Lord. I was desperately in need of some comfort—the kind only He can give.

The next morning, I awoke to the sounds of nurses rattling equipment in preparation for surgery. Soon, my children and my husband would be arriving to begin the waiting game. Much to my surprise, I felt the comfort and peace I had prayed for the night before.

The last words I said before being rolled into surgery were, "If I die, I'll be with Jesus. If I live, I'll see you in a little while. Either way, I'm a winner!"

SURVIVING THE BIG ONE

On October 11, my 48th birthday, I survived open-heart surgery and was given a second chance at life.

—Cherie Jobe

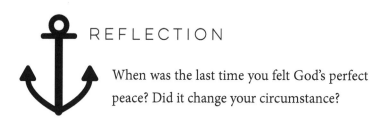

REFLECTION

When was the last time you felt God's perfect peace? Did it change your circumstance?

SURVIVING THE ENEMY'S PLAN

And we know that all things work
together for good to them that love God
to them who are the called according to his purpose.
For whom he did foreknow, he also did predestinate
to be conformed to the image of his Son,
that he might be the firstborn among many brethren.
Moreover whom he did predestinate, them he also called:
and whom he called, them he also justified:
and whom he justified, them he also glorified.

Romans 8:28–30

I had the opportunity to serve God during a Bad Hair Month! It started in the months leading up to November 2013. I had been extremely ill, hospitalized twice, and the doctors seemed unsure about what was really going on. Eventually, it was concluded that I needed to have my gallbladder removed.

I had not been at my present job for a year, so when I informed my employer that I needed to take off for the surgery, I was informed that I may not have a job to come back to. This bothered me a little, and I even toiled over the thought of not having the surgery. After praying about it, I was led to take the medical leave.

"I know you will be alright," my supervisor had said to me. "God has great plans for your life!"

Although tempted to argue with her, I heard myself saying, "Thank you. I accept that word."

Four weeks into my medical leave, I was in bed next to my husband who was making a pile from the Sunday paper he was reading. Noticing a particular page, God urged me to read it, so I did. It had nothing to do with me. Then I turned the page over.

There I found an advertisement for a women's conference—New Beginnings led by Cherie Jobe. I heard the Lord tell me I was to go to this conference. Laughing, I told my husband what had happened. I had no paycheck coming in, I was nearly certain that my checking account was overdrawn, and the ticket was $59. I said, "Lord, if you want me to go, you will provide a way."

All that week, I went back and forth with God. I *was* going to go. I *wasn't* going to go. I was a mess. As Friday came, I told my husband that I was going, even if I had to stand outside the door and listen. Checking the bank account, I found that we had $60. "Look at you, God!" I said. Now all I need is a ride. My husband was using our one car for work. Again, I turned this over to God.

As I headed toward sleep, the Lord told me that I needed to finish a shirt I had been making.

Now I was irritated. "Seriously? What more do you want? This can't be important," I insisted, but I got up and worked on the shirt anyway. Defiant, I told the Lord I wasn't going to wear it, and I finally went to bed.

My husband unexpectedly returned from work in time to give me a ride to the conference. His return woke me early, so I got up and finished the shirt at God's urging.

I arrived at the conference, not knowing what to expect. I sat by myself and told God I was ready.

The praise and worship were awesome as I lifted my voice with a roomful of faithful women. When it came time for a break, I went to the prayer table and asked for prayer to find a ride home. Then I returned to my seat, but I kept being drawn toward a young lady with a beautiful spirit.

I spoke to her at the lunch break, and we hit it off instantly. We talked about this and that, and then another woman walked up and said, "I love your shirt. When I get famous, I want you to be my fashion designer." I laughed and thanked her, then found out that these two women were together.

Next, the Lord gave me a message for the "shirt woman." He pushed me until I let him use me as his vessel. I told her that going forth, she should ask God to allow her to see herself as he sees her, not the way her family, friends or others see her. I explained that I saw a dark presence on her. It was so strong that it was affecting her physical characteristics. She confessed that she had a demonic presence in her life, and she asked me to pray for her.

I silently asked God to let this be his prayer. We prayed together, after which, she fell against a wall behind her. She stated that she felt free and that the presence was gone. I later found out that she had been involved in black magic and demonic forces.

You see, I thought I was there because my life was a mess. I thought this was going to be all about me. When I got home, I realized that God had allowed me to see his love in action. He had handled everything down to the minor detail of telling me what to wear.

The Lord asked me to do one more thing—call Cherie and tell her this story. I did, and we talked about how God used the conference to show me how much he loves us. I was amazed, blessed, and humbled by all of it.

We may not always know what's going on behind the scenes. So pay close attention to those bad hair days. We never know when they will be an intricate part of his love.

—Alva Bronaugh

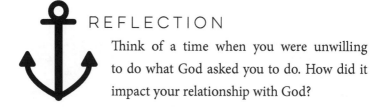

REFLECTION

Think of a time when you were unwilling to do what God asked you to do. How did it impact your relationship with God?

SURVIVING THE LOSS OF ALL MY FAMILY

"Come to me, all who are weary and burdened,
and I will give you rest.
Take my yoke upon you, and learn from me,
for I am gentle and humble in heart,
and you will find rest for your souls."

MATTHEW 11:28–29

I am an only child, spoiled, but never a brat. I grew up in Georgia and had an amazing childhood and family. My Dad and I were so much alike that we bumped heads a lot as I got older. We moved to California for Dad's job, just Mom, Dad, and me.

When I graduated from high school, I decided to move back to Georgia, and later my parents followed. I moved to

Nashville to finish college and returned to Georgia for visits. Dad lost his job there, so he partnered with his old boss in California; he traveled back and forth to visit also, of course much more than I did.

Dad was in the carpet industry, and in Georgia, he was a vice president over production. He was incredible when it came to his work. He was an expert in carpet production and machinery, and he held several patents related to carpet. But during the market downturn, Dad lost his job, which is how he ended up working in California and commuting back and forth. He and Mom were still married, and they made this work for some time. They were happy, and all seemed fine.

In December 2009, I went home for Christmas, and the holiday went fine. Dad's Mom had advanced Alzheimer's, and he was having a very hard time dealing with it. She was in an adult day care for a couple of hours a day at the time. Sometimes I went with him to take her there.

On December 30th, I went with him to pick her up, and we got into a huge fight—probably the worst fight we ever had. It was over how he treated her. I told him he was impatient and in denial, among other things, including telling him that I hoped he had someone to take care of him when he got old. I said that if I treated him like he treated her, it would be horrible for him.

Mom was still at work when we got back to the house, so it was just the three of us there. Dad and I were still arguing, and I decided that I'd had enough. I loved my dad to death, and I knew he would always be there for me, but in a mad frenzy I decided to pack my bags and go back to Nashville.

I said bye to my grandmother after throwing my bags in the

truck, then Dad came out and said, "April, I don't know why we fight so much, but I want you to know that I love you so much and am very proud of you." I looked at him and said, "Have a nice flight back to California," got in my truck and left.

Before I got too far down the road, God got my attention. I started feeling heaviness in my chest, and I felt I couldn't breathe. It was as though someone was saying, "You can't leave like this," and if I didn't turn around, I would suffocate.

So I turned around and went back. We were both crying as I said, "I love you so much," and he told me he loved me. It would be the last time I saw him alive.

On January 26, my birthday, I talked with Dad and felt good about where our relationship was. Then, on January 29, 2010, we had a major snowstorm. I was at work at Meharry. I called my mother who said it was snowing in Georgia too. She said she had been trying to call my dad and hadn't been able to get hold of him, but that was nothing unusual. I tried calling him, too, to ask about driving my truck in the snow, but he didn't answer my call either. Mom and I talked again, and she decided to leave work and go home.

Later, my roommate and I decided to pack up and go to a friend's house so we could all get snowed in together. I called to let Mom know where I was. My uncle answered the phone, and I knew immediately that something was wrong. My aunt got on the phone. I could tell she was shaky and didn't want to talk. She just kept telling me to go home, and someone would pick me up. She would not tell me what was wrong. I thought something had happened to my mother, so I screamed for someone to tell me what was wrong. Mom finally got on the phone, but she was hysterical.

My aunt finally told me that an ambulance had taken my dad and my grandmother to the hospital, and they were having to wait at home. I kept asking questions, crying and getting hysterical myself until finally someone said, "They are dead." Just like that.

My dad and my grandmother had died in the garage, and Mom had found them. My dad had been taking my grandmother to the car in the garage after he had started the car to warm it up. He had a heart attack and fell behind the car near the exhaust. He was found with his arms under his chest, facing my grandmother like he was trying to get to her. From the toxicology report, he probably died first from the fumes.

My mom and I got through a double funeral, and it was beautiful. Dad had done everything for Mom, but now, Mom and I had to start figuring out everything. We found out one of the two houses they had was in her name, and one was not. We had to walk away from the house they lived in within two months, so our grieving had to be put on hold while we decided what we would do.

Mom changed. She wasn't herself. She had just lost her husband.

The following April, I was home for a weekend, and I woke up to find her staring at me. "Mom, what's wrong?" I said.

It was like the dam broke in her, and she unloaded hysterically. She told me all of her questions and worries. "What am I going to do?" "Where will I live?" "I can't stay here." "I have nowhere to go."

I had never seen my mother like that because she was always

so strong, and it scared me to death. I called some relatives, and we took her to the emergency room. A psychiatric person came to evaluate her. They ruled her psychotic and wanted to send her to a hospital in Atlanta. I knew that she had not slept in days and had just experienced a great loss without time to grieve, so I asked them to give her something to put her to sleep and talk with her again in the morning. In that moment, I was going from being the child to being the caregiver.

After I fussed and argued with the doctor, they gave her a room and something to help her sleep. When she woke up, she was somewhat normal.

Between April and June, Mom did some bizarre things. I thought it was due to the loss she had experienced, and I talked with her about the two of us going to counseling, either together or separately. She actually went, but in July she began having really bad headaches and neglecting herself. She had always one to be put together wherever she went. She talked about odd things such as something that wasn't in the freezer that was supposed to be. Things were getting worse with her behavior, and she lost down to a size 0.

Mom turned 50 in September 2010, and I threw her a surprise birthday party to cheer her up and get her going again. At this point, all she wanted to do was sleep. I invited friends and family. She came to the party, but she wanted to go home as soon as she could. When I took her home to her condo, I found a mess. Her clothes were thrown around everywhere, and there were dishes all around. This was unlike her. I sat her down and asked her to please tell me what was wrong. She just looked at me. I was puzzled as to what to do.

I went home, and when I talked to her on the phone, her speech was slurred and slow. The headaches got worse. Although she was working through this time, it got so that she was late for work or would leave for lunch and stay gone for hours. These types of behaviors continued to get worse.

In October, I got a phone call from her co-worker who begged me not to tell her about the call. They were very worried about her odd behavior, including staring at her computer, wearing two different shoes to work and continuing to be late. On that day, she had arrived at work at 5:30 a.m. and sat in the dark until someone else came in at 8:00.

I told my boss I had to go, and I jumped in my car to drive to Georgia. On the way, I called a relative and asked them to get her to her doctor. I called the doctor's office and told them I wanted them to run a scan. I felt it was more than PTSD . . . maybe a brain tumor. They said she had been through a lot and was just depressed, but I had done some research and felt that it had to be something more.

I arrived in Georgia, and they had not done a scan. Her eye doctor said her eyes were fine and sent her on her way.

Now I was angry. I knew something was wrong and begged somebody to do something, and they wouldn't. Although she agreed to come back to Nashville with me and go to counseling, she awoke the next day and got ready for work. We got into a tiff, she went to work, and I came back to Nashville.

The next weekend, I was to come get her. My family thought she was over medicating, but I had them count her pills, and she wasn't taking them. When I got there, she was in bed with her sunglasses on. I tried to feed her a salad, but she was unable to eat for falling asleep between bites. Eventually, she just laid there like a vegetable. I was terrified. I had already lost my dad and my grandmother, and now I was losing my best friend, my mother, my world.

How could God let this happen? After all, we had been faithful for many years. I was so angry with God that I couldn't even pray. That part of my life had shut down.

I laid beside my mom all night while she shivered with cold. I piled blankets on her. Later, I found out she was having seizures.

By morning, she was unresponsive. My aunt helped me take her to the emergency room. After begging them to do a brain scan, a surgeon came in and told me they found a baseball-sized brain tumor. It was glioblastoma—the worse form of cancer you can have, and it was Stage 4.

"I would give her six to nine months to live," he said, "but I won't know for sure until I get in there."

I immediately went into "mommy mode." I told the whole family that we would not say the word "cancer" in her presence.

"When she comes to," I said, "we will tell her she had a tumor, and that's all we know. We will ease her into this."

And that's what we did. Even when the doctors came in, we talked outside her room. I virtually put her in a bubble.

After the emergency surgery, Mom was no longer the mother that I knew. They had taken out a large portion of her brain. She was now the child, and I was the parent. We soon realized that because of the size and location of the tumor, she had probably had a stroke, and her vision had been affected.

Quietly, I was still mad at God. I cried out to Him, "Why

her? Why now? *Why?*"

We decided to go to M.D. Anderson in Texas. She could not fly, so we took a road trip. I tried to make sure my mom had a good time while I was simultaneously on the phone with Vanderbilt, coordinating appointments, doctors, and treatments. I was also taking care of paying bills, communicating with family, making sure my job was secure—all of this at 26 years of age.

I have to say that we met some amazing people at M.D. Anderson. That place was wonderful. They treated my mother like a person, not a number. We found out that the original surgeon did not get all the tumor, so we made a treatment plan.

When I got her back to Georgia, I tried to keep her as independent as possible. I left her at her condo, knowing that there was lots of family around to visit and check on her. One of her sisters even moved in with her.

Meanwhile, I was living a double life. Around her, I acted happy, but behind closed doors, I fell apart.

We went back and forth to M.D. Anderson, and for all of 2011, she had treatments at Vanderbilt. Through the whole process, I did not want to talk with God. I cringed when people told me things about God and prayer. I was so angry at Him.

I continued to watch my mother dwindle. After surgery, she got shingles on her left side, and she began to lose her memory. She asked where Dad was.

At 27, I knew I was losing my only remaining parent. At M.D. Anderson, they went back in and got the rest of the tumor. She went through chemotherapy and radiation treatments.

Between keeping up with Mom's prescriptions, bills, her

condo and house in Georgia, her doctor's appointments, treatments, and my job, I was in a constant state of stress. I went from not talking to God or acknowledging Him at all to hitting rock bottom. Then I began to plead with Him.

"If you are there," I said, "help me know what to do. After all, you've allowed me to go through all this." As soon as I asked, He began to answer me.

In 2012, I quit my job at Meharry and got a new job in Maryland Farms in Brentwood. I moved Mom into an assisted-living home right around the corner from where I worked. I quickly realized that God had been with me all along, but I had been too stubborn to see Him.

Still dealing with all the details of life and the drastic changes in my mother, I decided that I needed to talk with Alive Hospice. I felt guilty that I could not do anything about her physical or emotional pain. I had to tell myself that I must do everything for her I could possibly do so that I would have no regrets. While she was in assisted living, I stayed with her a lot, even getting ready for work there, living out of a suitcase.

I told my new employers about Mom's situation and that I needed to be there for her because she would not be with me much longer, and they were very understanding.

Mom was in hospice care for about three weeks. At the beginning of that time, I pleaded with God to let me be with Mom when her time came. I had not been with Dad, so this was especially important to me. For those three weeks, I only left Mom to go to work. One day in what I consider to have been a small miracle, I was leaving for work, and Mom grabbed my hand and said, "Please don't leave me." Of course, I called work, and once again, they were supportive and understanding. They put together meals for us, bringing food two or three times a day for several days. Each time, a different person came and brought with them a card expressing their concern and telling me to stay as long as I needed to and enjoy every moment with Mom.

Finally, on Wednesday, August 15, 2012, I got up and decided to go to work. Something felt weird that day. I kissed Mom, then asked the nurse if I needed to call Mom's family to come for the weekend. The nurse said yes.

I also asked the nurse to call me if anything changed. I got the call at work from Alice Hospice at 9:30 that morning. Mom was dying. I had not been on the job but a few weeks, but I remember the women I work with surrounded me and got me out of the office as quickly as they could. One co-worker put me in her car while my boss jumped in the back seat and called my aunt and uncle. Another co-worker grabbed the keys out of my purse and followed behind in my car.

On the way, I remember calling my best friend Shelly in California. "It's time," I said, "and I am not ready for this." She immediately jumped on the first flight out to be with me, and for that, I am forever grateful!

When I made it to Alive Hospice, I tried to get to my mother's room as quickly as I could. It felt like it was a thousand football fields away. When I got to her room, I fell by her bedside sobbing, holding her hand, and telling her just how much she meant to me.

Within the hour, the chaplain came into the room to pray with us. While I knelt by my precious mother's bedside, still sobbing, the chaplain began to pray. At that very moment, my mother opened her eyes, looked at me, and took her last breath.

As I look back at the journey I have taken so far, I see God's hand throughout, even when I didn't want to recognize it.

From the very beginning of my journey, God…

…made me turn my truck around to tell my dad for the last time that I loved him.

…gave me the gut feeling that something was wrong with my mother when everyone else told me I was wrong.

…gave me the chance to take care of my mother for two years before she passed, when the doctor only gave her six to nine months to live.

…gave me the ability to find M.D. Anderson in Houston, Texas, where she had surgery no one else could have performed—the second her doctor had said she could never have, removing the remainder of the visible tumor.

…let my mother always recognize her family, telling us how much she loved us, even when the doctor said she would forget.

…provided me a job next-door to her assisted-living home.

…answered the biggest prayer I will ever pray, letting me be by my mother's side as He took her home.

It is 2014 now—four years since my dad's and grandmother's passing, two years since my mother's passing, and two years to reflect on my journey so far.

As each day reminds me that they are gone, there are also reminders that they are still here with me. Recently, I started to really miss my mother and wish that I knew she was watching proudly over me. I recently moved, and as I went through boxes of things, I came across a card I had never seen before. It was a Christmas card. When I opened it and saw whom it was from, I became overjoyed! The card read, in my mother's handwriting, "You deserve the best! I love you, Mom".

I know there will still be ups and downs on my journey, but I know I will see my family again someday, and I know God has me in His hands.

— APRIL JOHNSTON

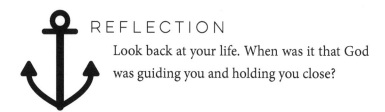

REFLECTION

Look back at your life. When was it that God was guiding you and holding you close?

SURVIVING CHILDHOOD ABUSE

Yea, though I walk through the valley of the shadow of death, I will fear or dread no evil, for you are with me; Your rod and Your staff, they comfort me.

PSALM 23:4

The best thing I can say about my childhood is that I survived it. Born in Columbia, Tennessee, I lived with Mom and Dad in the Elkton and Ardmore areas with two sisters and a brother. Growing up was not easy. My father was not the provider he should have been. He worked until I was in 4th or 5th grade. After that, he was disabled. He was turned down for disability, and this made him very unhappy so he had to find work somewhere.

We were on food stamps and aid-to-children. Dad handled all the money and decided what was paid and not paid. I can remember several times when he spent money set aside for the electric bill and food to buy alcohol. During these times, we'd end up with my grandmother. Mother worked at a truck stop until she hurt her back and had to stop; other than getting something new every once in a while, our clothing came from the kindness of strangers.

Although it was an abusive marriage, my parents were married 43 years. On several occasions, my dad almost killed my mom. One night when he was beating her in their bedroom, I tried to get him to stop. He told my brother and me to mind our own business. We didn't have a phone, which was one way my dad controlled us. Dad never let Mom learn to drive. At one time, a teacher helped Mom with her education, but when Dad found out, he stopped that.

No one ever reported what was going on. I lived in a family where we did not talk about such things. We were told, "What goes on behind closed doors, stays there." My grandparents knew what was going on, but I didn't tell anyone. I think it still goes on like this today. Even today, my husband deals with domestic situations, and he will come home and say, "Why do people deal with this?"

I was frightened, and I withdrew inside myself. I watched a lot of TV—shows like "Little House on the Prairie" and "The Waltons"—and I fantasized that my life was like that. Dad would punish us by spanking us with a belt. One time my twin sister wanted to go to our grandparents' house to do some schoolwork, and he would not let her. She pitched a fit, and he

SURVIVING CHILDHOOD ABUSE

dragged her out the door by her hair. In one house where we lived, there was no plumbing. To take a bath, we had to go to a neighbor's to get water and bring it home.

One time when Mom was at work, I had taken a sponge bath when Dad came into the room and caressed my breast. He said, "Kiss me," and I refused. My sisters saw this and asked me, "What are you and Dad doing?" I said, "Scuffling." This was when I was about 11, and it did not happen again. I have not confronted my dad, but I have told my husband. A cousin molested me when I was 13 years old. I did not tell my mother or anyone. It was one of those things where you did not tell. This went on until I was around 16.

After graduating from Giles County High School, I attended Columbia State College (CSC) to get out of Elkton. I worked a full-time job in a cabinet shop while going to school. It was stressful, but nothing compared to the stress I had grown up in at home.

I met my husband-to-be while I was at CSC. He is from Germany, an army brat who became a citizen when he was five years old. He had lived in Germany, Colorado, and Texas and decided to go to Columbia State when he got out of the military. He saw me on campus and told himself, "I'm going to hook up with her." One day he approached me and asked if I wanted to get a soda. Although I'd just had one, I said yes, and we walked back to the student union for a soda. We sat and talked over a soda, and the next time we met, he brought me home. Since I was a cautious person, I was clutching the door and thinking, "If he makes a move, I'm out of here." Thankfully, he was someone I could trust.

We dated for a year. During that year, he had to go to Germany for three weeks. We thought that time would be our time to figure this out. When he returned, we got married. It was March 1988. I was 20 years old. I did not finish school, but lived in Franklin as a police officer's wife. We found we were going to have a child so we started looking for a house. We moved to Murfreesboro in 1990, and our son was born on my birthday that year.

We have stayed in Murfreesboro since then, and I have worked a variety of jobs, most of them related to customer service. I taught school a bit, but it was not God's plan for me. As much as I thought I wanted that, it was not for me. I worked at Kroger and Toys 'R' Us. I loved holiday season at Toys 'R' Us. We worked our schedule out together. I would get off work and come home, and he would go to work. Our second son was born in 1993. We decided that we would use daycare, so we shuffled kids and schedules.

I think getting married at 20 was my way of escaping, but my life has been so much better. I kept in touch with my mother, mainly to be sure she was okay. Dad continued to beat her up. She tried her best to fight back.

I joined a Celebrate Recovery twelve-step study class at church. It helped tremendously. Following that, I went on the Emmaus Walk, which also helped me deal with my childhood. The leaders there prayed with me and counseled me. Although I had accepted Jesus Christ at 12 when the Elkton Baptist Church youth group attended a youth conference, I really had no idea what a relationship with Him was until I went to Emmaus.

SURVIVING CHILDHOOD ABUSE

Celebrate Recovery, the Emmaus Walk, and seeing a counselor were very helpful, but I still struggle with self-worth. To this day, I compare myself to other women. I truly wish I had confidence. My life verse is Matthew 6: 25, which basically says, "Don't worry about tomorrow, because tomorrow will take care of itself." I still worry, though, because I still want to be in control.

God protected my boys and me when we were involved in car accidents in 1994 and in 2005. He was also by my side in July 2003 when I discovered a lump in my breast. On the way to the doctor we were in another minor car accident. When my doctor examined me, she said the lump was only a cyst. I insisted that she order tests because I knew my body, and I knew something wasn't right. After the ultrasound, mammogram and lumpectomy, I began treatments in September, with chemo every three weeks until December. The treatments were awful, and I had nausea all the time, but my hair did not fall out, and the Lord and I got through it together.

—Brenda Gibson

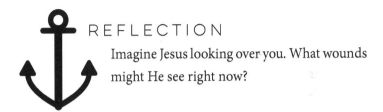

REFLECTION

Imagine Jesus looking over you. What wounds might He see right now?

SURVIVING A CHEATING SPOUSE

*For the which cause I also suffer these things:
nevertheless I am not ashamed:
for I know whom I have believed,
and am persuaded that he is able
to keep that which I have committed
unto him against that day.*

2 Timothy 1:12

I met my husband at church when I was about 17 years old. He seemed like a good guy. He was close to his parents and was very kind. We dated for about three years and married when I was 21. We got along well. We both worked, and we traveled some. Things seemed good.

About six years into our marriage, we had our first baby. He passed away as an infant. After that, our relationship declined. Initially, we clung to each other and turned to God.

After another six months or so, I became pregnant again. The pregnancy was difficult, but I gave birth to a healthy baby girl. Our relationship was back on course again, and things were going pretty well, although I had some issues with postpartum depression.

I became pregnant for the third time. Once again, I endured a difficult pregnancy before giving birth to another healthy girl.

This is when things really began to get worse.

I went back to work on night shift. My husband did not want to care for the new baby, and he had started to withdraw from me. His story was that he had cared for the first baby, and he did not want to care for this one.

Regardless, we cruised along with our routines, caring for two children and working full-time jobs. We were in church all this time, never missing. My husband was not the spiritual leader of our home even though he was in church three times a week. He never wanted to read the Bible or pray.

The busyness of life moved us along, and when our oldest daughter was in her early teens, my husband met a friend. He began to have lunch with the friend, which I really didn't mind at first. He had not had a friend during our married life, and I encouraged him. I was still working nights, so he spent that time with the girls.

As time progressed, he began to spend more and more time with this guy. Their relationship grew while our home life became more and more unhappy. He was verbally abusive to the point that the kids noticed. It was stressful for all of us and was a sad time. He was getting closer and closer with this guy. When I asked why he wanted to be with this guy, he made up an excuse. The kids, who were 16 and 11 at the time, told me that Dad thought they didn't notice that he left the house after they were in bed and come back early in the morning before I got home from work. He was spending the night with this person.

In the meantime, my brother- and sister-in-law who lived across the street from us noticed him leaving. My brother followed him and discovered where he was going. This went on for a good year. I did not know what to do or who to talk to. We were still in church three times a week. The situation escalated as my husband became more and more involved with the guy.

I felt so much shame and felt I had no one to talk to. I began to look online for help. I googled "straight wives, gay husbands". I was looking for anything to help with what I suspected. Embarrassment kept me from talking to my friends, but I found a lady to email, and she turned out to be a great resource for me.

One night when the kids were gone, the two of us went out to dinner. He asked for a divorce, saying that he did not want to be around me anymore and that he wanted out of the marriage. I was not surprised, as I had felt this was coming, but I thought we wouldn't really deal with it until the kids were grown. He never admitted he was gay at this time, even though I came right out and asked him. So I hired a private detective who found that all evidence pointed to the fact that my husband was having an affair with this man.

My husband left a credit card lying around, so I went online to see what he was using it for. Sure enough, he was spending money at gay bars. He was buying liquor, even though we had never drunk. I printed receipts and had other evidence from our computer that he had been looking at pornography.

My husband finally filed for divorce, and I was served. He was still denying he was gay, even though I confronted him with all the facts I had gathered. He broke down and cried, then finally admitted that he "had feelings for him" but was still in denial.

I knew.

There were gay bars, gay bookstores, gay websites and so on. He cried and cried, I think because he had been caught, not because of the divorce. We got the divorce on grounds of adultery, although he never admitted his homosexual lifestyle when confronted with all the evidence.

As we went through the divorce there was a lot of battling. This was all traumatic for our children. Once when my older daughter and I were visiting a college campus, he had a guy over to the house when the younger daughter was there. She saw the two of them in the hot tub, and she knew from their interaction that it was not right.

It has been six years since the divorce. In the midst of it all, I started the healing process and a new job. I went to a counselor, stopped, and recently have begun to go again. Every now and then, I feel the shame and embarrassment, and I struggle with anger over what he has done to the kids. I believe he hid behind the marriage and the church for years, and he still hides behind the church. He lives two lives—gay and straight.

SURVIVING A CHEATING SPOUSE

For me, moving on is a work in progress. I cling to my faith, believing that God never left me. There are still days when I struggle, but various Bible studies that God has put in my path have helped me so much. One book that was helpful for me was *Things I Learned from the Red Sea*.

My advice for others is this: Don't be ashamed for what someone else does. Don't hide behind a mask. Reach out for help.

—Shirley Cassidy

REFLECTION

Reflect for a moment upon the suffering you have survived. Has the suffering brought you closer to Jesus or father away?

SURVIVING MENTAL ILLNESS

Be still and know that I am God.

PSALM 46:10

When major depressive disorder threatened to take me under, I experienced what I think of as a very dark night of the soul.

Misdiagnosed with a seizure disorder and improperly medicated for nine years, I went into the neurological surgery floor of the Vanderbilt University Hospital in a wheelchair, having disintegrated over the past month of medical leave from my job. During that month, I cried out to God to heal whatever it was that was sapping my very will to live. Because I believed that God had the power to heal, I decided that my lack of faith or my inadequate prayer life kept me spiraling downward.

As if this wasn't frightening enough, I was admitted to the hospital to undergo final tests to rule out multiple sclerosis.

When the myelogram came back clean, the roving herds of interns and residents that roam the sterile halls of Vanderbilt Hospital began to notice how often they found me crying. It wasn't until they asked that I realized that I cried at least once a day.

My dad chose this time to fill me in on what he knew about his family's history of mental illness—specifically mood disorders. It turns out that his mother and her mother, along with most of his siblings, suffered from depression, manic-depression and/or obsessive-compulsive disorder.

The medical team—after many rounds of questions—asked if I would agree to be moved to the psychiatric floor. I was willing to try anything that might help lift the veil of darkness that had enshrouded me for too long.

When I arrived on the locked floor, my primary care nurse came in to ask yet more questions. Although I was apprehensive, I immediately sensed that she was someone I could trust. I confided in her that I had one major fear; I was afraid that if I admitted that I believed in God, the medical experts would chalk me up as someone who was using faith as a crutch and try to take that away from me.

This angel of mercy assured me that they absolutely would not think of doing that because they had seen people of faith benefit greatly from their beliefs. Once I knew I was safe, I allowed myself to participate fully in the program, which included individual and group therapy, medication changes, and community participation.

This being 1988, I was allowed to stay in the hospital long enough to get me safely off the wrong medication and onto new, appropriate medication for a genetic predisposition to major depressive disorder and severe anxiety attacks that mimicked petite mal seizures. Even though I had actually had several grand mal seizures, they subsided when the rest of my life came into balance.

During all of this, there were times when I did not know how to pray. At these times, I know that the Holy Spirit heard my groaning. As I began to heal, my faith rose up to meet me, and I began to see light at the end of the tunnel. I came to believe that God worked in my life through my insightful mental health team, my father's willingness to share his own history, appropriate medication, therapy, plenty of creative outlets, time spent with precious friends, His Word, His Spirit, going to Him in prayer myself, and leaning on other believers who held me up in prayer day and night.

Regardless of how dark our nights, they cannot compare to His future glory. I have had low times since 1988, but when they come, I use one of the tools He has given me, often replaying one of the many times His mercy and grace have shined a light into my life. Try memorizing a verse that brings you comfort, such as "Be still and know that I am God" or "Peace, be still." If you practice saying it when you are calm and peaceful, it will come to mind when you are not.

—Cindy Phiffer

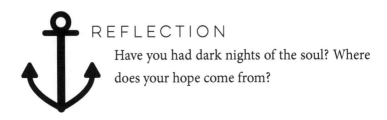

REFLECTION

Have you had dark nights of the soul? Where does your hope come from?

SURVIVING THE LOSS OF TWO CHILDREN

You keep track of all my sorrows.
You have collected all my tears in your bottle.
You have recorded each one in your book.

PSALM 56:8

I was born and raised in Honolulu, Hawaii, and at two days of age was adopted by a wonderful family who brought me into their home and loved me. As I grew older, I got to know my biological mother and other family members, but I felt the rejection because I was given away rather than being kept by her. She had other children, and I questioned, "Why was I tossed away?"

As I grew up, I found the Lord and realized that it didn't

matter that I was adopted; my family loved me, and God loved me. It took me a long while to accept that love, but eventually I did.

I married at the age of seventeen because I was pregnant with my first child. I had a rotten husband, and after two years, we divorced. I moved to the big island in Hawaii and raised my son there. I remarried and had two more boys. My oldest son was with me until around nine years of age, then he wanted to be with his grandmother. She was able to afford more things for him, and he felt he would be happier with her. At the age of 17, he moved to San Diego, California, with his girlfriend. They planned to be married, but two weeks after his eighteenth birthday, he was killed in an automobile accident. He had fought with his girlfriend before he got into his car. I had lost my first son. The most wonderful thing during this awful time was that two days before he died, he called to tell me he loved his brothers and me. He asked me to bring the flowers, leis, and other traditional things for the wedding. He asked to speak with his middle brother, who is the mischievous one in the family. I told him his brother was asleep so he told me to tell him, "Please be good because it is not fun to be bad."

The next day, I went to church. A lady sang a beautiful song. After that, we were sitting in a circle, and a lady said to me, "Let me pray for you." I said, "No, I'm okay." I had not been saved for very long at that time and was not used to someone praying out loud for me. She insisted, so I said okay. All my lady friends and the pastor's wife were there. We held hands, and she prayed. I remember her words, "I pray that God will lift you up and hold you in His arms for the crisis that is about to come." My pastor even wrote those words down and gave them to me. Around midnight, my phone rang. It was my son's grandmother telling me he had died in an accident. That woman had prayed for me for a reason.

My son's body was brought back to Honolulu, and my pastor and my best friend went with me. We were going to the mortuary to see him but before we could go back there, my pastor came out and said to me that we could not go back to see Peter, it is a closed casket. That is God! I had said to Him at various points in my son's life that I could never look at my son in a casket, so He made sure I did not have to. Wow!

I returned to the big island, and I continued to go to church. My husband at the time did not go, and he made it difficult for me to go. He might take my car keys away, or if I started to walk to church, he would drive alongside me and pull a gun. He did not want me to go to church, but I continued to go. Once, when I was at church, my husband called and was yelling at me where the pastor and his wife could hear. He was angry that I did not have his dinner on the table. I had prepared it for him but it was not on the table, so I left to go home. I was very fearful because I knew he was drunk, and my pastor and friends were scared for me too.

My husband took one look at the meal and said, "I am not eating this slop!" He demanded that I sit down. Then he began to yell and wave a beer bottle around. I ran to the sliding glass door to get away from him, but when I got outside, I knew that the neighbors could hear so I went back inside and sat down again. My knees were shaking as he stood over me with the beer bottle by the neck as if he was going to hit me with it.

Then suddenly he said, "You know I cannot hurt you. God has angels all around you for protection." He got up, went straight to the bedroom and went to sleep. I called my pastor immediately and said, "Pastor, the strangest thing just happened." I told him what had happened, and he said "Praise God, that is exactly what we prayed for you—that God would place His angels around you."

After that, I was able to get away from the verbal and emotional abuse. We divorced after almost 20 years of marriage. I was still struggling with feelings of rejection and unworthiness, and I felt that God could not forgive me.

I moved to Honolulu with my sister (all three sons were grown by this time), and I got a job teaching beauty school, which I loved. During this time, I met my present husband who was a friend of my brother's and was in the army. He was a real, down-home country boy from Maryland and was just about ready to go back to Fort Campbell, Kentucky. Within three months, we found we could not live without each other, so we came here and got married. He retired from the army, we move to Maryland but I just did not want to live there. It was too far away from my home in Hawaii. Finances also got in the way. His retirement wasn't much, and I worked in a salon not making much. We decided we would go across country driving an eighteen-wheeler. I got my license and learned to drive too. We did that for 10 years. For two years, I cried from the homesickness, but after a while, it became fun, and we got to sightsee and experience a lot of the country.

Then, about the 12th year of driving, my oldest son called and asked if his daughter, his girlfriend, and he could move here to our house because he wanted to make a new life for his family. Jobs were scarce on the island, and they were struggling to pay their bills, never able to get ahead. My husband and I talked it over, and we decided to help them. We paid off their debt and told him they could come here. I would have a granddaughter! I told him they would have to get married to live in our house, and he said "Never mind then." My son was one you could not tell what to do. If it wasn't his idea, then he would not do it.

The day after I said that to him I was walking through the house, and I heard an audible voice of the Lord say, "Let them come, and I will take care of the rest." I called my pastor to say, "Could it be?" He said, "If you heard it then it was the Lord." He advised me to tell my son to come, not mentioning that the Lord told me. My son had grown up in the church but had strayed. So I apologized and said, "No strings attached. You can come." There was nobody in the house because my husband and I did not get home more than about every three months. We were on the road. They came, and a few days after they arrived, my son was walking past me in the living room. He stopped and asked me if I still attending a certain church. I said yes, and he said they would like to go with me. He turned the corner and went upstairs, and I said, "Yes! That was God."

They came back to church. He became involved in men's ministry, and my now daughter-in-law got saved. Immediately after being saved, she came home, took her clothes to the other bedroom and told my son they would not live together until they were married. On my birthday, I took them on the General Jackson where he proposed to her. A couple of months later they married in a beautiful ceremony in my backyard. They became pillars in our church. After sometime, they became homesick for Hawaii but both my pastor and I told them we didn't think it was time. They decided to move anyway, and they moved to Las Vegas where there are lots of Hawaiian people. It is called the "ninth island" because so many go there to live. Her best friend and her family lived there. They moved in August of 2004. My son had a really good job here, and when he moved there, he got a good job there with the Wynne Hotel's laundry facility, running their maintenance department. He was proud of that job, and so were we.

On Mother's Day, they sent me a ticket to come see them. I missed my son and granddaughter so much. When I got to their little apartment, my son said, "Come, Mom, and see my new bike." I opened the door and saw this green "crotch rocket" type bike. It hit me like a ton of bricks in my spirit, and I said "Son, sell that bike." He said, "Oh Mom, it so cool." But I insisted that he sell it. That was in May. I found out he was having strange encounters with God, such as turning around in the road and seeing darkness. He had strayed from church. I told him he must turn back to the Lord.

In July, I was walking through Roses Department Store and had a sudden desire to call him. I did, and he was changing clothes at work getting ready to leave. I told him I loved him and he told me he loved me, too, and appreciated all I had done to care for both my sons to help them get to where they are today. I asked him to call me that night so that we could talk, and he said he would. Thirty minutes later, he was killed in a motorcycle accident. He was cremated after a service in Las

SURVIVING THE LOSS OF TWO CHILDREN

Vegas, and we took his ashes to Hawaii. I returned to Las Vegas with my daughter-in-law and granddaughter to clear out the apartment and have a yard sale to sell his things.

The night after he died, I was angry at God. I questioned, "Did I not do enough for you? Did I not pray enough, give enough, sacrifice enough?" I cried out to him, really upset.

I came back to Tennessee, and I was angry. I was here but wasn't myself. My husband would say, "I really want the old Cindy back." I'd say, "You got it!" But I was ugly and mean. My son had been my best friend. We were very close. We could sit and talk about anything.

After all that, I was going through life angry. God was trying to love on me but I just wasn't there although I was in church. One night in a dream, I had this sudden awesome exciting feeling—a sense of pure love. I had never felt anything like that before.

My pastor had had specific people praying for me because I was mourning. One Sunday at church, I could not stop crying. I was going to leave because the tears were flowing like a waterfall. One of the ladies who had been praying for me stopped me to say, "Where are you going?" I said, "I cannot stay. I must go home." I hurt so badly. I had not laughed for months. I tried to push her aside. When she hugged me, I just fell down from weakness. She got another lady who had also been praying for me, and they took me into the library. She said, "God told me there would be a time would I have to do something for you. It is not me. It is God. I am going to hug you because God has been trying to hug you." She was a large black lady, and when she hugged me all I could feel was her body and mine. It was as if I could feel something coming into me. After that, I was still crying. When I pulled away, she said there is one thing God wanted her to do. I said okay. She said, "It is not me, it is God. Take one step to the right, then another step to the right." I did what she asked, and suddenly the sky seemed to open up for me in light, and I started to laugh. I couldn't stop laughing. They prayed for me again, and we returned to the sanctuary. A friend saw me and said, "Wow, you look great Cindy. We were really worried about you. You were dark but now there is a difference."

As Christians, I believe we are supposed to mourn but we are not to grieve. I loved my son so much.

Shortly after the death of my oldest son, my youngest son Barry got very heavy and tried to commit suicide. He was sitting in a car with a knife in his hand. He called me while I was at church, and one of my friends grabbed the phone and prayed for him.

He was living in Las Vegas at that time, but soon moved back to Hawaii with his family. He started going back to church. God touched him, and today he is a pastor.

I always prayed that my children would worship God but never dreamed one would be a pastor. Now he and his wife are doing great things in the ministry.

God is faithful, faithful, *faithful* even when we are not. He is always there.

—CYNTHIA DEAN

REFLECTION

Take a moment to listen to your heart.

The source of my pain is _____.

God has turned my

(source of pain) _____

to (source of joy) _____.

SURVIVING A BRAIN HEMORRHAGE

Give all your worries and cares to God for He cares for you.

1 Peter 5:7

My name is Jenni Feldhaus, and I survived a subarachnoid brain hemorrhage. It was on the right side of my head, just below my ear. Evidently, it had been bleeding for years while I thought the headaches I suffered were migraines. It had clotted itself off on numerous occasions.

One Monday morning, I awoke with a headache that lasted all day. This one was different as it was in the back of my head where the migraines had always been more on the top and front. I also realized I could not think as well. I was at work preparing an invitation for an event. A friend was sitting there with me, and I said to her "I just can't think."

Tuesday, Wednesday, and Thursday went by. I felt worse but just trudged on, as women tend to do. On Friday night, I got very sick, hurting, and vomiting. My husband Henry took me to the emergency room around midnight. They gave me fluids and pain medications, then sent me home around 2:30 a.m. We kept thinking it was a migraine, but the migraine usually lasted two or three days. This was different, as it was now going on six days. On Saturday, I got up and felt weak, but the pain was lessened. Henry and some others did some family activities but I didn't feel like going so I stayed home. They got in, we talked, then went to bed.

When I got up on Sunday, I felt like a champ. We went to Huddle House to eat, and I can remember seeing someone I knew there. I began to get sick again, and they took me home. That is the last I remember.

At home, I had tried to get up, but passed out. The remainder of the story is told by my husband, Henry, because by this time I had "left the building!"

[At this point, Henry takes over the telling of the story.]

We learned that the vertigo was a typical side effect of the headache. On Saturday, I called our friend who is a physician's assistant (PA) and who had also been working with Jenni that week on the headache. He said that something else was going on, and he wanted to do a CAT scan. He called a local doctor who said it could be done at his clinic. We had scheduled that for Monday morning. But the "wheels came off the bus" on Sunday. Our daughter was home from Knoxville, and we had been working on my new TiVo setup so that we could record the Super Bowl the next week. When we went into the bedroom to check on Jenni, she was in the floor where she had thrown up and was seizing a little bit. She looked like she had aspirated a little, and we found out later she had.

We put her in the car and sped off to the local emergency room. We had called our PA friend on the way, and he insisted, "Get a CAT scan now. Get it now!" He told the ER doctor that he was available by phone but he was also on the way. They wanted to repeat fluids, put in an IV, and do what they had done on Friday night. There was a nurse there, who also works for our PA friend, and she kept telling them, "If he said do a CAT scan, then you should get it done!" She took charge, and the ER doctor finally agreed. It didn't take long, and they came busting back in a hurry and told the doctor something I did not completely understand, then everyone came out of the woodwork. They wanted to call the helicopter but the weather was bad, and I told them they would not be flying tonight because of visibility. As a pilot, I knew that. I said we needed an ambulance to go to Vanderbilt University Medical Center (VUMC). When we called Vanderbilt, they said to intubate her. Now, I knew something bad was going on, and we had to get her to VUMC. They kept going back and forth about the helicopter, and I insisted that we needed the ambulance to go *now*.

We were still thinking this was still a migraine issue. Our daughter had decided to go on back to Knoxville so she was on I-840 when I called and told her to turn around go to VUMC where she could be sure no time was wasted in getting Jenni admitted. She and Jennifer have the same name, same insurance card, etc., and I thought it would expedite things if she could get there quicker. I rode in the ambulance, and by the time we got there, they had a room and were ready for her. Another nurse who knew us was there, so she stayed with Jenni when they took her back and told me to step out. By this time, our PA friend was there but we still did not know what exactly was happening.

I barely got to the waiting room when a doctor came out and told me her heart stopped, then asked me if she had a heart problem, was she a diabetic, and what else was wrong with her. They were trying to get her heart back. Finally, they let me go back, and Aubrey (our PA friend) went with me. They kept insisting something was going on besides a migraine. Aubrey told them "no" she does not have those issues. They said her heart was like a fatigued muscle. We later found out that her heart had been working so hard dealing with the aneurysm that it was simply overworked. If she had not has such a strong heart she may not have survived.

They were trying to chase down all the other symptoms. Aubrey could talk their language, and he insisted, "This one is worth saving. You are supposed to be the best. You must find out what is wrong!" They had an entire team working on her. Aubrey and I both were in and out all night. They had her hooked up everywhere…at one time about 16 tubes here and there. Basically, it was all to keep the heart pumping and at rest, and to keep the blood pressure low so that if another event happened, it would not be fatal. That went on through Monday, then in the afternoon, the heart started to get better. They had not done any tests on her head yet because they needed her heart to recoup. By Tuesday afternoon, they did another CAT scan. Through all this (which she does not remember), she was kept sedated. Tests on Tuesday revealed the leak in the back of her head. The doctor then told us that there was a new procedure that could be tried where they go into the head with a coil and fix this. They wanted to continue letting her rest until the doctor who does the procedure could get there on Wednesday afternoon.

When he got there and looked at her and the tests, he said, "Yes, we can do this." He said it would be a six-hour procedure. It was something new; he had done the procedure on the heart but he felt he could fix this brain hemorrhage with the same procedure. They would shut off the blood to the brain, shoot this coil in there, then start the blood pumping again. The key was that she would be up to twenty minutes without blood to the brain. She could wake up with less memory, and we didn't know what other complications might happen.

He said, "I can do this. You take care of the praying end, and I'll take care of this end." I said, "Okay", as that's what I'd done since I got there. Jennifer was taking an anatomy class at the time, and she brought her book to the hospital. We had gone through the brain section, and the doctor had traced the entire thing for us, showing us exactly where everything was and what he would be doing. I sat there as in a trance, going through every vessel of her brain and praying.

Since Monday night, we had insisted that they do what they do best and take care of the situation. Even when the doctors kept insinuating, "The husband does not understand how serious this is." I repeatedly told them, "Yes, I do. I knew she was in bad shape, but I also was confident that I could handle the situation and anything else with the family; they just needed to do their job and do it to the best of their ability.

The surgery was set for Thursday. They explained that they would not be able to send out much communication since the procedure was very meticulous. After a late start, they took her back at around 10:00. I was sitting there among 20 or so others in the waiting room with my eyes closed. At around midnight, I saw my daddy and her daddy—both deceased doctors—walk by and give me a sign that all was okay. I got out of my chair and felt a complete sense of peace. I told my family, "I'm ready to go eat." They looked at me like I was crazy but I said, "It is going to be okay. I'm hungry." We stayed in the cafeteria and were gone an hour or longer, then we returned to the waiting room. Around 3:00 a.m., they came out and said it was over and we had a successful surgery.

It was a wait-and-see situation the next 24 hours, to see how much memory, etc., might be affected. The doctor told me the first two hours of the surgery was rough, but then I told them that around 12:15, I felt it was fixed, and he said, "That's exactly right." I told him what had happened, and he told me that the first attempt at the coil did not work and they had to wait, then go in again and were worried that damage might be done. But then, on the second attempt—around 12:15—the blood started to flow. They explained that we would not know about what damage was done until later. So much had to happen in this procedure to get the blood flow working again like it should. I said, "It is going to be fine." The heart came back beautifully.

Jenni was in intensive care for about two weeks. Jenni

finally woke up and asked, "What happened?" She asked them where she was and when they said Vanderbilt, she thought she must really be sick…and she was…but she did not have to go to Stallworth or anywhere for rehabilitation. They called her the "February Miracle".

When Jenni was able to go home to Shelbyville, Tennessee, during the last week of February, people were lined up, ready to bring food and wait on us for several days. The doctors acknowledged that our "higher power" was responsible for Jenni's recovery. My faith and general optimism is how I knew Jenni would be okay. We've learned that 50 percent of people who have this type of hemorrhage never get to the hospital, and a large percentage of the survivors of a brain aneurysm have permanent disabilities.

We know that prayer and God's provision is responsible for Jenni's recovery.

— Jenni Feldhaus

REFLECTION

Who are your prayer partners? Remember to share your specific needs with them so they can cover you and stand for you before our Father when you are too weak to stand for yourself.

SURVIVING ANOREXIA AND BULIMIA

Be strong, vigorous, and very courageous.
Be not afraid, neither be dismayed,
for the Lord your God is with you wherever you go.

JOSHUA 1:9

I grew up in a loving, Christian home. We went to church every Sunday, and when the time came, I was active in my youth group. I would describe my childhood as a "Leave it to Beaver" home. Then, at the age of 20, my world came crashing down around me. My father—the first love of my life—died.

After that happened, my whole way of living was different, including my home. I completed my bachelor's degree and moved to Florida just to get away from everything. While there, I gained a lot of weight, became depressed, and forgot about how much Jesus loved me. I had begun to despise myself, and I struggled with very low self-esteem.

Not knowing what else to do, I decided to move back home after only eight months. I was broken; I was empty, no matter how much I continued to eat; and I had allowed my relationship with Jesus to starve to death. During this most vulnerable time, I met a man who took an interest in me. This was hard for me to believe because I did not think anyone could love me. After all, I knew I was fat, and I felt extremely ugly—disgusting, even. We started dating. After only three months, he said he would propose to me if I lost 30 pounds. So that's just what I did. I lost 30 pounds in two short months.

We got married four years later, and everything seemed great…at least for a while. Then, one decision at a time, he began to take away my control. He would not allow me to see any of my friends, which made me resentful and lonely. If I wasn't with him, I could not be with anyone else. During this time, a horrible thing happened. I was brutally raped, and I became pregnant. My husband was sterile, so we knew it wasn't his baby. He was furious, and he accused me of cheating on him. I decided to have an abortion, hoping to find a way through this nightmare.

I found out a month later that he was having an affair. When I confronted him, he told me he was going to end it with her. This went on for months, and during this time, it seemed I had no control over anything in my life. I decided it was time for that to change.

I started exercising more and eating less. What I did allow

SURVIVING ANOREXIA AND BULIMIA

myself to eat, I purged. I became anorexic and bulimic, hoping my husband would love me if I were skinny. People started telling me how thin I looked, and that just added fuel to the fire. Those "compliments" hastened my downward spiral. My addiction was one thing that I held onto in the divorce.

Seven months after my divorce, I ran into a godly man named Phillip. We had known each other in college, and we started dating. After a few weeks, he told me his friends and he thought I looked sick. They were concerned about me and were willing to walk with me through the difficult road to recovery. With his support and the relationship I started to renew with Jesus, the healing process began. Phillip and I got married, had a beautifully healthy baby girl—a miracle in itself because I did not think I could get pregnant because of the damage I had done to myself—and we are still happily married today!

As soon as we got married, we started going to church and getting involved. Today Savannah is 13, and we are in relationship with Jesus. Looking back, when I thought I was all alone, Jesus was there carrying me through the rough times. He never left me, even when I turned my back on Him. He is always there for us, no matter what.

— JENNIFER DYE

REFLECTION

Think about someone you know who is hurting. Ask God to give you the right opportunity to reach out to them.

SURVIVING A
NEAR-FATAL WRECK

I will lift up mine eyes unto the hills,
from whence cometh my help.
My help cometh from the Lord…
The Lord shall preserve thy going out and thy
coming in from this time forth,
and even for evermore.

PSALM 121:1–2, 8

My name is Josh Carney and I survived a near-fatal car accident. Monday, February 24, 2014, started out like a normal day. My wife Amy usually works 12-hour shifts so I pick up our son on Mondays. Amy and I had actually met for lunch that day in an unusual way. We met at First Community Mortgage to sign papers for a mortgage refinancing.

I went back to work, got off at the normal 4:00 time, went to my son Mason's pre-school and picked him up. I had planned a trip to the cell phone store in Murfreesboro that day to swap some equipment and would take Mason with me. We came home first, got his diaper bag, and left for Murfreesboro. I was thinking we'd go to the store, then maybe have some dinner before returning home. Arriving at the AT&T store in Murfreesboro, we had a 45-minute wait. While waiting, we played around the store on all the tablets, games, etc. Mason had a really good time doing this and was well-behaved. The clerk who helped me with phone equipment asked what I did. I replied that I am a tech guy, repairing phones, computers, etc. Somehow, the conversation got around to church, and she asked me where I attended. I told her we were between churches now. Amy and I had gone to a small church here in Shelbyville. The Pastor left so we were looking around. My mother and father had invited us to World Outreach Church the week before, and since we'd never been there, we thought it a good idea. So, before I left the AT&T store I told the lady we planned to be there the following Sunday. As you will see, that never happened.

I remember walking out the door, lifting Mason into his car seat, fastening his seatbelt, and giving him his iPad to play during the ride. I tightened and checked his seatbelt like I normally do and noticed that the chest harness was pretty tight so rather than loosening it, I just moved it down a little. Nothing unusual.

SURVIVING A NEAR-FATAL WRECK

As we left the store, I called my brother Adam around 6:30 just to see how the new phone sounded and to tell him rather than meeting him to eat, we'd go on home since traffic was a mess that night. Mason repeatedly asked to stop at McDonald's but because of the horrible traffic, I passed up one and then another. That was the most traffic I'd seen in Murfreesboro in the four years I'd been driving over there. For a Monday night, it was very strange. It was packed and seemed very unusual for that night of the week. I told Mason we'd go on toward home, then stop for food.

Mason was playing his game as we headed down Highway 231. At Christiana, I saw a policeman on my side with his blue lights on. I slowed to a stop and just assumed that something must be going on on the other side of the divided highway. Mason said something to me, and I glanced up in the rearview and saw a full-size pickup truck coming that was obviously not going to stop.

It was a Chevy Silverado going at a high rate of speed, and I knew we were in trouble. I braced on the steering wheel and just hung on. From that point, it seemed that everything was in slow motion. I could see the glass particles flying by my face. I saw him drive through my car in slow motion, saw a tire go by my face. My seatbelt held me as our car spun 180 degrees, and when we stopped, we were facing the opposite direction. I got out of the car and immediately felt like I came back into my own body. I was in a rush to find my son then, but the car seat was not in the car, neither was my son. There was no back door; the car was a big mangled mess. The whole side where Mason was riding was ripped open. You must see the pictures of the car. It was completely destroyed. No one should have survived that.

I went around the car looking for Mason. He wasn't there. No one else was around for about five minutes. I felt completely alone. I thought I'd lost my son, that everything had come crashing down upon me. I was yelling his name, listening for him. I was trying to hear whimpering or crying, but couldn't find Mason. A tractor-trailer, which had also been hit by the same truck, was sitting there. I looked up at the driver, pleading, "Have you seen my son?" He just shrugged his shoulders and kept sitting there. It felt like an eternity when I could not find my son.

Then a lady got out of her car and approached me. She asked what happened, and I told her I'd been hit and couldn't find my son. Another lady came up, and I begged for help to find my son. I was afraid of what I would find, but there was not a trace. One lady stayed with me, and one went looking for Mason. Then I noticed my arm. It looked like a snake, obviously broken. I took off a top I had on and wrapped my arm to hold it in place while I looked for Mason. A first responder came up and began to help the lady look for Mason. I told them not to bother with me, just please help find Mason. I had looked everywhere, under the car, where the trunk had been, under the truck beside us…

Then, the lady yelled, "I found him!" I said, "Is he alive?" She didn't answer, but just pointed to over where he was. I went to him and found him bleeding from the ears and mouth with his eyes closed and not responsive. The worse possible thoughts entered my mind. I went back to my car and said to

SURVIVING A NEAR-FATAL WRECK

the lady, "I know there is nothing I can do for my child but pray. Would you hold my hand, kneel with me, and pray for my child?" We did that and another lady came up and prayed too. I am convinced that prayer changed the way things were going.

The officer then told me that the helicopter was coming and would be there in seven minutes. It seemed like forever to me. Lifeflight landed and took Mason to Vanderbilt University Medical Center while an ambulance took me to Murfreesboro. Here I was, not knowing the status of my child and in a different place.

My brother Adam was called. I had used one lady's cell phone to call Amy to tell her Mason had been ejected from the car and I didn't know if he'd make it. Adam and Amy showed up minutes later. The officer told Adam and Rachel that Mason had a strong heartbeat. That's the first indication I had that Mason was still alive. I hadn't asked because at that point, I didn't want to know.

I was in the emergency room beside a guy that had been killed in a motorcycle accident on I-24 about the same time as my wreck. Mom and Dad and everyone else had gone on to Vanderbilt to be with Mason, and my brother stayed with me while I had my broken arm set. They had given us a status update when the helicopter landed, and at that point, Mason was stable. I told the folks in Murfreesboro that I could not stay, and they were great to get me fixed up with an x-ray and some morphine. Then, I was out of there so I could go to Mason. My hand was broken and my right arm was shattered. It was a major deal for my arm, but I had to get to Nashville.

I didn't know what to expect. Adam and Rachel were trying

hard to keep everything positive, saying that everything would be alright. I was scared and in shock and pain and did not have the courage to go into Mason's room. My family told me he was in a neck brace and pretty beat up. At that time, we knew he had a significant, traumatic brain injury; ligaments in the neck and spine were separated so that he could not hold his head up; and frankly, only a thin piece of ligament was holding his head on. He was literally decapitated on the inside. That was really scary. They had him immobilized in the bed and hooked up to breathing machines with a pain pump. To see a two-year-old child like that was terrible, but he was still alive.

Amy was with him and never left him. I went in when I felt I could but was not able to handle it for long. That same day, I went back to Murfreesboro to have my arm re-wrapped. It was turning blue because the wrapping was too tight. They had told me that I could wait a while to have surgery on it as long as it was in a splint. I wore that until I felt that Mason was doing better, then I had it operated on.

A little at a time, Mason began to come around. He was on so much pain medication, he was out of it mostly. He would open his eyes some, but stared into space. He couldn't do anything (walk, eat, stand, laugh, etc.). All he could do was whimper or cry. This was just a shell of our son.

We prayed and prayed. Pastors came by, many people prayed. Reporters wanted to interview us. After several weeks, we were told we would have to go to Atlanta to an in-patient rehab facility. Mason had become conscious, but was extremely frustrated. The only thing I remember him saying before we left for Atlanta was "I'm sorry." As a parent, that was hard to hear. I went through every emotion. I was angry that I allowed him to be hurt but thankful that he was alive. You look at your child like this and it puts everything into perspective.

Probably what kept me from completely losing my cool was being thankful that he was not dead. It all could have gone the other way. It was way bigger than me. I felt that I was not in control at all. It wasn't about me. In myself, I would have tried to find the guy in the truck. I would have vented my anger in some way. But I knew this was beyond me. What we did that day (praying for my child at the side of the road at the worst time) was the best thing I could have done. Instead of my seeking revenge, God intervened and let me know I was not in charge and could not "do" anything. Thoughts such as *my marriage is over, my family will be devastated, I'll never be able to work again, I will not be able to go forward* ran through my head when my child's life was on the line. Then all of a sudden, I knew that I would not be able to go forward on my own but I would give it to God. On the side of the road, I gave it to God. Not knowing whether Mason was alive or dead, I gave it to God. From that moment on, I knew I was not in control. God came in and took the situation for me.

We were in Atlanta for three weeks or so, and we saw many improvements while there. The brain activity started to show up, and he could move around. It took a while before he could walk. He did have a feeding tube in for a long while which was painful. When it came time to take that out (which is a painful thing) they told me I could do it or the nurse could. I said I would do it. I wanted Mason to look at me and know that I was helping him get rid of this painful thing. His voice changed when that was in, and it is still different than before.

A couple days after the wreck, I asked my father-in-law to get my personal effects from the car. The only thing he found in the back seat was my Bible, which had been in the trunk. It was lying on the seat where Mason's car seat was. When I got the Bible back and started to look at it, it immediately fell open where it has been creased at one place—Psalm 121—which explained all that happened. It says, "I turn my eyes to the hills from whence my help comes. My help comes from the Lord. He watches over me and protects me in my travels (going out and coming in)." It gave me faith right away, immediately. Here was God telling me He was protecting me. You are fine today, and you are going to be fine. I believed it and still do. That psalm says it all for me.

Mason is physically doing well. He is in a lot better shape that he could have been. I prayed he would be able to live his life without machines. We could deal with other things. He is a typical two-year-old boy. We know that we are totally blessed to have him with us. I know God picked my son up from that car and set him in the median of the highway still in his car seat. The angels were around him that day.

I would say to others, don't try to go through this yourself. The Lord had come to us in this situation through other people who have surrounded us. Our community and many Christ followers have come to us, prayed with us, and helped us in many other ways. This has given us hope that we can overcome significant things. My wife and I made the decision that we

SURVIVING A NEAR-FATAL WRECK

would not go back to work until Mason is well. We have not left his side, and God has provided. He has pulled a blanket of safety over our lives.

I have always been a giver myself and love doing that because there is no greater blessing than to be able to give. So, I had a hard time being on the receiving end, but I have found that I can be a blessing to others who have come forward to help us. I never thought I would need help nor did I think other people would help me. I learned that I was totally wrong. All people are not all about themselves; there are many givers out there. This experience has allowed me to swallow my pride and accept the grace of others. It has been a blessing to be on the receiving end, because I know now that you cannot outgive the Lord, no matter how much we try.

—Josh Carney

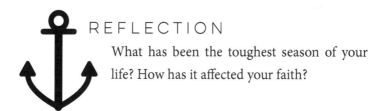

REFLECTION

What has been the toughest season of your life? How has it affected your faith?

SURVIVING A TORNADO

*Fear not for I am with you; do not look
around you in terror and be dismayed,
for I am your God. I will strengthen and
harden you to difficulties,
yes, I will help you; yes, I will hold you up and
retain you with my right hand of rightness and justice.*

ISAIAH 41:10

On April 10, 2009, our home was destroyed by an EF4 tornado that came through Murfreesboro. Our daughter Tori, two of her friends, and I took cover in a closet, our safe place, as we are instructed to do when there is a threat of tornado. As we sat there in the dark, trying to make light of the situation, it wasn't long before we heard the "train," felt the house shake violently, and ultimately explode around us.

It grabbed us out of our safe place and tumbled us through a cloud of grey dust, deafening us by howling winds, splitting wood, and clattering debris, then slamming us down somewhere out in our front yard. We found ourselves buried under the rubble of what had once been our home.

In less than 10 seconds, my life was forever changed.

As I tumbled through the monstrous wind tunnel, I felt my back pop, and the most intense pain shot through my entire body. My L2—Lumbar 2—vertebrae shattered from the force of the wind as it twisted me into unnatural positions. In addition, my left clavicle or collarbone, all the ribs on my left side, and my sternum were all broken, and my lungs were bruised. Muscles and nerves were stretched and torn in my back and shoulder.

Praise God, the girls walked away with no broken bones and no stitches needed! Kristen stepped on a nail as she climbed out of the rubble and had to have that treated, and Laura's foot was stepped on and hurt by one of the men who tried to get her out from under a mattress and framed wall under which she was pinned. They were all scraped and bruised, but they were alive and unbroken!

My husband Brian was in Nashville, praise God, so he was spared. Had he been home, there would not have been room in that closet for all of us, not that he would have even attempted to take cover.

My back surgery took 13 hours, including time in Recovery, and I was in the hospital for 11 days. About 11 days later, I had another surgery to repair my collarbone.

SURVIVING A TORNADO

Although I'm alive and able to walk and move, I'm in physical pain every day. It is taking forever for my back to heal. I'm never completely comfortable in any position. The most frustrating issue is this wonderfully vague, chronic condition called fibromyalgia, which is usually brought on by a serious illness or traumatic injury. I'm still trying to wrap my head around "chronic," but I just don't get it.

What I *do* get is that God is allowing this *affliction* in my life, which Beth Moore has helped me understand better. According to the *Encarta Dictionary*, *affliction* is "a condition of great physical or mental distress." There are many biblical accounts of people with afflictions. Some of these are Hagar, Jacob, the Israelites, Hannah, Job, and Paul.

We may all be able to relate to having some type of affliction. We have either had an affliction, we have an affliction, or we will have an affliction of some sort. Some are short-lived, and some last indefinitely. I have had a hard time admitting that I have an affliction or "a thorn in my flesh," so what I'm sharing with you today is current, fresh, raw.

In Psalm 25:16 (NIV), the psalmist says, "Turn to me and be gracious to me, for I am alone and afflicted." When our affliction surfaces, there is a sense of loneliness that accompanies it. Even though I read about people with fibromyalgia, talk with other people who suffer from it, and see that Lyrica© commercial 20 times a day, when I have a flare-up, I feel like no one could possibly know exactly how I feel. Because my symptoms are not visible—I don't break out in a rash, my tongue doesn't swell up, I don't get cross-eyed—I feel like others might think I'm just making it all up or that I'm just lazy or seeking attention. These feelings cause me to withdraw a little (or a lot) until I feel better or take enough medication that I don't care anymore.

Affliction involves submission. Either we submit to the affliction or we submit to Jesus Christ. Since Satan is the author of affliction (2 Corinthians 12:7), we need to be aware of what we are actually doing when we submit to our affliction. God does not give us afflictions as punishment. He allows our afflictions and sometimes leaves them with us to remind us of His sufficiency.

Grasping this truth is not easy. But we can't just be hearers of the Word without putting it into practice. We have to stop everything and spend time with Jesus. If we don't "Be still and know that [He] is God," we become vulnerable to being stopped in our tracks.

I know. I was an activity addict. I felt like if I wasn't constantly moving—serving, cleaning, working, feeding kids, driving kids, getting things done—I was doing something wrong. Then one day, I was multitasking—driving and praying. "God," I said, "I don't feel like I'm being used enough by You. I want more of You and to feel Your presence more in my life. I want to have a story that will interest others. And please make a way for me to be home with Tori. She needs me during her high school years, Father. It's such a crucial time in a young person's life. Of course, we do have debt to pay off, so I'll just keep working until You show me otherwise."

On Good Friday, 2009, God answered my prayers. Of course, I hadn't imagined that answer coming in the form of a tornado, but He heard my prayers and answered them,

SURVIVING A TORNADO

plus some I hadn't even known how to utter. We lost all of our worldly possessions that day, and I lost my health. But we have seen firsthand what is promised in Romans 8:28 (KJV)—that "all things work together for good to them that love God, to them who are the called according to His purpose."

For most people, that day is a faint memory. I live it every day—not in fear, but in my body and my soul. It changed my life, totally for the good. I have an affliction I don't understand, but it keeps me focused, and for that, I am so grateful. God is teaching me beyond what I could ask in the midst of all this. Most of all, He is teaching me to keep my eyes on Him and rest in His peace that passes understanding.

—JUDY REED

REFLECTION

What is your current thorn-in-the-flesh? How are you addressing it?

SURVIVING CANCER

*Now to him who is able to accomplish f
are more than all we ask or imagine,
by the power at work within us.*

EPHESIANS 3:20

Steve and I married in July 1997. My children Ashton and Codie were five and six. Steve adopted them when they were 12 and 13. My husband and I had a good life. I had been a Christian as long as I could remember. We went to church, gave our offering, and did everything Christians are supposed to do.

In May 2009, things began to change. Steve's company shut down, and he invested in a mortgage broker business. Ashton decided to find her biological father and then chose to live with him. The mortgage business took a huge hit, and we lost more than half of our income.

I started to question God. "Why are you letting this happen?" I cried. "We are good people who are faithful Christians." I got *angry*. I refused to pray because I felt God didn't listen to my prayers. When my husband prayed, I wouldn't even close my eyes.

But I continued to go to church. Our Sunday school class started a Read Through the Bible in a Year program. I decided to participate. After all, it was the Christian thing to do. Little did I know how God would use this to change my life. As I read the Bible, my faith grew.

When the mortgage business was good, it was very good, and we lived well. Whatever was needed, we just wrote a check. We made a lot of really bad choices when it came to finances. Once the mortgage industry changed, so did the way we lived.

On November 2, 2011, at 12:00 p.m., we lost our home on the Rutherford County courthouse steps. But it could have been worse. We could rebuild in time and live simpler lives. After all, home is where the heart…and our family…are. That house was just a building.

Steve contacted our pastor and told him about our situation. Our pastor gave us a gentleman's name. This man later became our landlord. He met us at one of his properties. We loved the house, thinking it would be perfect for our family. He told us what he charged. Steve said there was no way we could afford that. The landlord asked us what we could afford, and he agreed to accept that amount.

SURVIVING CANCER

On November 9, 2011, Steve and I both went to work. We worked for the same mortgage company. On a conference call with our corporate office that day, we were informed that our office would be closed, and November 15th would be our last day. We were in a daze.

On November 11, Steve went to have a colonoscopy. He has one every two years because colon cancer runs in his family. One brother died at 33, and another one died at 47. His father was diagnosed with colon cancer at 47, had his colon removed and lived to 61 before the cancer returned to take him.

When the doctor came out to talk to me after Steve's procedure, I took one look at his face and I knew. The tears started, and he confirmed that Steve had colon cancer. I went into the bathroom so I could really cry. While I was in there, I also called Momma because sometimes nobody understands like your momma.

As soon as Steve saw my face, he said, "I have cancer, don't I?" The doctor explained what needed to happen next and asked if we had any questions. Steve asked if he could have a cigarette. The doctor said yes, adding that cigarettes did not give you colon cancer. That day, we scheduled as many doctor's appointments and CAT scans we could cram in by the 15th.

After leaving each appointment, we called our pastor giving him an update and asking him to pray with us. We told our children and then our families.

On December 5th, Steve had surgery to remove the part of his colon that was riddled with cancer. The surgery went well. The doctor said that he got everything and that the lymph nodes were negative for cancer. We praised God!

For five days, everything went well. Then Steve got to feeling bad so they inserted a nasogastric (NG) tube in his nose to drain the stuff that had built up in his stomach. Even though this was quite painful, Steve started to feel better as the week went on.

On December 16th, he was discharged from the hospital. Over the following eight hours, discomfort progressed to unbearable pain, and we headed back to the hospital where he was readmitted with an abscess. They needed to operate immediately, as this was a life or death situation. We asked everyone for prayer, including our pastor who was with us through this roller coaster ride. He prayed with us and the doctor, which was a true blessing.

The surgery was only to take 45 minutes. I watched the clock, waiting for the time to pass…and it did. First, an hour, then an hour and a half, then two hours. Finally, 2 hours and 23 minutes later, the doctor came out. He told us that it had been necessary for him to call in another surgeon. He said Steve's intestines were the worst he had ever seen. When the doctor touched the intestines, they simply fell apart. One of the nurses later told us that she went home and cried that day, sure that Steve would not make it.

The doctor told us that *if* Steve made it through the night, he would have a very long, hard road ahead of him. I had thought that the surgery would fix everything, so I was unprepared for this news. In fact, after I heard the phrase that started with *if*, I didn't hear what he said next about him having two milestones.

After we stopped crying, the kids and I went home. When

SURVIVING CANCER

I finally got there, I prayed, "God, I am not asking You to save Steve or fix Steve, but I am asking that Your will be done, that the outcome will glorify Your name and that I would have the strength to deal with the outcome."

The next morning, I went to the hospital where I found Steve sitting up in bed in the ICU. He was not only alive, he was doing well! When I saw the doctor, he was smiling ear to ear, obviously relieved that Steve had made it through the night.

It had certainly been a full, life-changing 17 days. After 4 surgeries, Steve's stomach would no longer hold together on its own. They added some strips across his stomach in order for it to heal. He also had to have a wound vac. Steve had gone from 231 pounds when he first entered the hospital to 178, his lowest point. We spent 97 days in the hospital altogether and 6 months in a hospital bed.

There were days that Steve felt so bad he would ask God to take him to heaven to get him out of his pain. Each time, God was there with and for us. He never let us down. We had much support from our church and our friends.

In July 2012, Steve was able to do a take-down procedure; the bag came off. Complications led to two more surgeries, making the total seven surgeries in eight months. The immediate danger was over, but the long, hard road was still ahead of us.

In September 2012, our unmarried daughter, Ashton, told us she was pregnant. This was very hard for us, as Christians, to face. We wondered whether we had failed as parents or God had let her down. We worked through those feelings, accepted the reality, and moved forward.

On January 17, 2013, my precious mother was diagnosed with cancer. I spent every weekend with her, taking care of her.

On April 8th, Ashton went into labor. On the 9th at 8:17 p.m., my beautiful, precious Sophia Marie was born. I took a picture and had it sent to my mother so that she would know that mother and daughter were doing fine. Seventeen minutes later, my mother went to be with Jesus. God had given us Sophia's sweet new life to hold onto as we let go of my dear mother.

I learned many things throughout these trials. Our fortune is not here on earth but in heaven. Life is best when it is simple. It is okay to say "cancer," it's not contagious, and you don't have to be afraid of it. I learned not to say to someone lying in bed with cancer, "It could be worse. Think of all the children who are suffering with cancer." When it is you or your loved one in that bed, you really don't care because you could die and that is the worst it could be. I learned that celebrating Christmas and New Year's in a hospital isn't bad when you're surrounded by friends and family. And you can really decorate a hospital room if you try!

During all of this, God has taken care of us in every way. He knew what we needed and when we needed it. Steve is still cancer-free. His days are still hard, and he has not been able to return to work, but he's alive! Our trials are not over, and we still struggle, but we still rely on God.

We hope that at some point in time, we have blessed someone by helping them hold onto their faith. We pray that someone might be able to make their struggles a glory to God instead of getting angry with Him. Because of our trials, my

SURVIVING CANCER

faith in God is stronger, and I love Him more, so I thank Him for those trials. By God's grace, I'm a survivor.

—Karren Welborn

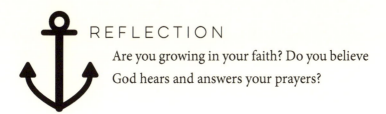

REFLECTION

Are you growing in your faith? Do you believe God hears and answers your prayers?

SURVIVING A CHANGE IN PARENTING PLANS

I can do all things through Christ who gives me strength.

PHILIPPIANS 4:13

The day I found out I was pregnant, I immediately knew something was wrong. I thought I was miscarrying. The very next day, I was in the doctor's office, and they confirmed the pregnancy but told me there was an 85-percent chance I would miscarry. I was dead-set sure that I would not miscarry. I didn't dwell on that. Lots of people in my church were praying, and we stayed firm that this baby would live. At six weeks, we went for the ultrasound to see if I had miscarried. They said, "If we see a heartbeat on the ultrasound, then you've not miscarried, and chances that you will miscarry after that drop to about 2 percent." As soon as the wand was on my stomach, we saw a heartbeat. The doctor and I both screamed with joy, and I was coming up off the table excited!

After that, my pregnancy was normal. In fact, it was a wonderful pregnancy. I loved being pregnant, didn't gain much weight, never felt bad, didn't swell up, and never got sick. At eighteen weeks, we went for the gender ultrasound, and after several days of waiting to hear, the doctor told me our son had a cleft palate. We didn't tell our family immediately, because we were trying to process what they told us.

They called us back for a confirming ultrasound, and all we were told was that he had a bilateral cleft palate. We kept telling ourselves, "It can be fixed. It can be fixed." The doctor told us there was something different about it, but we didn't know what. We went every week for an ultrasound, and it became more and more apparent that there was something more wrong. They referred us to Vanderbilt University Medical Center.

The biggest concern was that because Christian's cleft was so unusual and severe (affecting his mouth and nose), he would not have a clear airway to breathe. They were not optimistic that he would live.

They told us that his deformity was so unusual that they could not tell us very much. We were given a list of "possibilities." He could be blind, deaf, mentally impaired…you name it, and it was on the list. We tried to learn all we could about the various deformities they gave us, but as devout Christians, we believed that we could handle whatever was given to us.

I worried, but not more than any new parent would. It was our first child, and we were nervous. I never really accepted

SURVIVING A CHANGE IN PARENTING PLANS

the thought that he might not live. At the last ultrasound, he yawned, so we knew that there was a clear airway. They snapped a picture, and it was beautiful. The doctor said that doesn't mean 100 percent that he can breathe, but to me that was a huge relief.

One of the things about Christian was also that his amniotic bands were attached to the placenta in such a way that they could not see the right side of his face. We didn't know this until after he was born, but it kept us from seeing the "worse" side of his face.

After he was born, we learned that he was blind. That was the hardest thing. We had been thinking about the cleft and the fact that it could be fixed, so we had not thought about blindness. We had not known about the severity of his condition because there just was not good information…so many what-ifs and much uncertainty.

Christian was born on February 18, 2011. I was so relieved that he was alive. He was evaluated and tested for several days. I'd had a C-section so was trying to deal with everything while recovering from my surgery. The first few days are still a blur. After about 4 days (he had a feeding tube), they decided to insert a permanent feeding tube because he would not be able to take a bottle. He also had an open place on his head that had to be closed with skin. Again, I was numb and don't think I even processed what all was happening.

On the day of the surgery, we stayed with him up until they took him back for surgery, then we were with him for the remainder of the day. As we were getting ready to go home, I left the NIC Unit (Neonatal Intensive Care Unit) to pump since

I was breast-feeding. While I was gone, the doctor came in and told my husband that Christian was blind and nothing that could be done about it. When I returned, Chris was crying. That was devastating, the way the doctor did that. He didn't wait for me to come back into the room or anything. We didn't even know this man (an ophthalmologist), so it was horrible.

Christian was in the hospital for four weeks, and the entire time was awful. We did see that he was going to live, could breathe, and was functioning. There were so many doctors and much speculation. They showed me a CT scan of his brain and said one side was bigger than the other, an indication that he would be mentally impaired. During this time, specialists were coming and going. They were telling us so much about what would be required to care for him (medical equipment needed, many surgeries to follow, etc). It was overwhelming.

Finally, we were so relieved to bring Christian home. He had, and still has, the feeding tube. It will be removed once he has the cleft surgery and is able to eat on his own. We did the best we could for a while. Chris went back to work after a week. I had to return to work after my leave. It was difficult to find someone to keep him, but we had one friend from church who is a nurse, and she helped us through the first few months. Now we have a private-duty nurse. Those first months were hard just trying to figure things out.

The first few times we went out in public, some people stared and others asked, "What is wrong?" I had never been one to stare, so this was new to me. Once when a friend was with me, she said, "People over there are whispering about you." When I looked at Christian, I didn't see a baby with a cleft

SURVIVING A CHANGE IN PARENTING PLANS

and no eyes, so this was hard for me to comprehend. One time when I had covered him with a blanket, a young man came up and asked to see my baby. I tried to prepare him by telling him that my baby was different, that he was blind, and that he had a cleft. He insisted, so I let him see Christian. He gasped and covered his face, horrified. Although he apologized, that incident hurt so bad I went home and wept.

Not all people are unkind. Many are very kind and thoughtful, encouraging us and praying for us. One mother asked if I would speak to her little boy. She said, "My son thinks your little boy is hurting. Would you explain to him that your son is not in pain?" Of course, I was happy to do that, and after I spoke with her son, he felt better. He asked what he could do for Christian. I told him that from now on when he sees someone with a disability, be kind and talk just as he would talk with a "normal" person. After that, I knew I would do my best to go about educating people about disabilities.

I started writing articles for the paper here in town. It was just a way to advocate for the disabled. It wasn't meant to be just about Christian, but for the disabled in general. The series of articles was called "Just the Way You Are". One article that got a lot of attention was after I had read a touching story to Christian about a mama and baby polar bear. People began to recognize us in public and to remark about the articles. I try to write two a month with information about how to approach a person with disabilities, how families can get support or help, and how to treat a person with a disability.

I can understand children who ask questions or say awkward things because they are only mimicking adults. I like to explain to kids and help them understand. It upsets me when parents don't correct children or ignore their comments or questions rather than explaining in a kind way. Kids have to be taught, and I so want to teach everyone around me so that Christian and people like Christian can be accepted.

Christian goes to Special Kids (SK) in Murfreesboro three times a week, and we use that as an opportunity to educate people about his disabilities. We do fundraising for SK too. We are researching schools for Christian for when he is older. We are meeting people who are helping us so much. I've met a lady in Franklin who is with the National Federation for the Blind, and she is helping me know how to raise Christian so that he can be all he can be. I've met another lady who is blind and is a music teacher. She went to Tennessee School for the Blind, and she is a great help to me. I really enjoy reaching out to these people and becoming part of their network.

Christian has a normal life expectancy. He is starting to crawl, pull up. He is ahead of target for blind kids. Special Kids does so much for him. He is progressing in leaps and bounds.

Being chosen to parent such a special child has been a rollercoaster. God comforted me all during the pregnancy, and I just knew it would be okay. There was a time, however, that my husband and I both were angry, even furious at God. I would say to God, "You could snap your fingers and make my son see! Why won't you heal him? It's not fair! I don't deserve this, and neither does he!"

One day when Christian was about 4 months old, I was at work and was rambling in my head at God. A song on the radio about God's mercy—"Blessings"—got my attention, especially

SURVIVING A CHANGE IN PARENTING PLANS

these lyrics: What if trials of this life/Are Your mercies in disguise? I heard God say, "You asked me to let him live and I did, so why are you complaining?" It got my attention, and I have not had more pity parties. I quit feeling sorry for myself. Rather, I see that I am blessed to be chosen as Christian's mother.

I think there is one thing special-needs parents can agree upon: There are so many things we need but we will not ask for them. We forget that there are so many people who want to help. So, I'd say to these kind-hearted people, "Force your help upon these parents!" It is so easy for us to say, "No, I don't need anything." But if someone says, "I'm bringing dinner," or "Here is $50," I can just respond with "Thanks." I don't know any parent of a special-needs child who doesn't need something. I so appreciate generous deeds such as a gas card appearing in the mail, those who show up to babysit so Chris and I can go out, or a grocery gift card thrust into my hand when I least expect it.

One way I give back is by encouraging others to stand on what they know. The Bible says: God knows the plans He has for us, to prosper and not for harm. (Jeremiah 29:11) There were times when I didn't believe He would prosper me, but I learned that if we stand in the truth, even when it doesn't look like we will prosper, God will prove Himself faithful and truthful. He has proven himself over and over to us and to so many others who have gone before us.

I understand those who doubt that God can use them to share His Good News. After all, I am only 25 years old, and I have lived in the small middle Tennessee town of Woodbury, Tennessee, all my life. But I have been in day care work for nine years. I love being around the fun and innocence of children. I am also in my second year at Nashville School of Law. I dreamed of being a lawyer since I was little. It is probably the second hardest thing I have ever done. I want to practice disability advocacy and special education law, help people with Social Security disability applications, and assist people to get where they need to be. I've been through these things, and I want that JD (law degree) so that I will have the authority to help others get things done. My husband Chris and I have been together for 10 years and married for 4.

—LACEY BUCHANAN

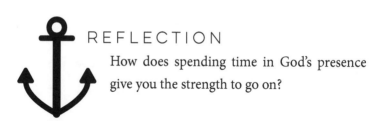

REFLECTION

How does spending time in God's presence give you the strength to go on?

SURVIVING ABUSE AND ABORTION

If any man be in Christ, he is a new creature.
Old things are passed away and all things are become new.

2 CORINTHIANS 5:17

I was born to a 16-year-old girl and a 17-year-old boy. We lived in a little garage apartment behind my great-grandmother's house. I was adorable, precious, and loved. I am the oldest of four girls.

As a very young child, I was surrounded by "love," if love means getting a lot of attention. When I was five or six years old, my great-grandfather—my mother's grandfather—stuck his hands down my pants while everybody was at the kitchen table. I remember telling my Mom. She and my Dad were in the front seat of the car, and I was in the back. We were on our way to my father's parents' house, which was always a safe, happy place to be. I said, "Mama, Granddaddy puts his hands in my panties." She said, "You tell him he is not allowed to do that. You tell your Granddaddy that your Mama said no!" My father didn't say a word. Even years later, when I confronted him with it, he responded as if he had never even heard the conversation. I don't know if my Mama or Daddy said something to him, but my great-grandfather never did it again.

This was never discussed again until sometime in my adult life when I talked about it with my sisters. Years later, I learned that he was a child molester, a rapist who had abused my mother and others. Eventually, in counseling, I dealt with it. I questioned my Mother's actions. Why were there times when she actually let me spend the night? Why would she have put me in danger like that? The therapist told me that my Mother may have seen herself as a victim but never saw me in that way.

One result of this abuse is that my antenna is up all the time. I have a daughter, and I am always tuned in to danger.

I survived Granddaddy. We all loved him. We thought he was "gross" or "sick." I didn't really know about sex but I knew what he did wasn't right. I guess we were supposed to love him because he was family, but we were really there because of Granny.

My parents had many financial stressors and lots of challenges. I was a "Daddy's girl." I adored him, still do, and I always felt I needed to defend him. He had a temper, he was jealous, and my mother may have been flirtatious. I have to be careful, because in my mind I thought my mom must deserve this because my daddy was so wonderful. I thought he wouldn't do this if she didn't deserve it. I really couldn't wrap my head around this.

I grew up seeing violence in our home. When I was about six, we lived in this little house. Daddy was a firefighter, and Mama stayed home. Then we moved to a bigger house, which I thought was a mansion. When we couldn't afford it anymore, we moved back to a smaller house and that is when the violence started. I think it was the stress of life. My father was 26 years old with 4 children. I guess my world was still a happy one, and I thought we had a happy family.

One particular event sticks in my mind. I was around 3rd grade, maybe 9 years old. Dad was choking Mom. He said, "Go to your room." Mom said, "Go to the Swansons," so I went across the street to their house. I played with my friend, Sarrah, and I never told them that someone was getting hurt. I knew I needed to leave my house for a safer place, and somehow I was able to act like everything was normal when it was definitely far from that. Bizarre, huh? We already knew about keeping secrets. I didn't tell anyone—not my teachers or anyone.

Once I begged, "Daddy, please don't kill my Mama!" He stopped. Sometime along the line, I got it in my head that if I was good enough, sweet enough, he would stop. I thought we would be happy, and no one would get hurt. Things weren't ideal, but they were still good in my world, or so I thought. There were plenty of good times. I didn't think others—like our neighbors, for example—had anything to hide. Now I know that we all have things in our lives we want to hide because we live in a fallen world.

We ended up moving back to the bigger house. We went to church where my father was choir director. He started having an affair with a woman in the choir. I was mad at him. Mom and Dad separated, divorced, and he remarried, all in one year. He didn't marry the woman in the choir but another woman who lived next door to his mother. He ended up calling my stepmother his "other mother."

When I was in the 8th grade, I was going to a Baptist school, and my mom was dating too. There weren't many kids at that strict school who came from divorced parents. There was lots of talk about sin, hell, and what I had to do to be good enough. Then I'd go home, and Mom had men in her bed.

During this time, I had a dream I'll never forget. I was sitting on the front porch on a beautiful day. The sky cracked open, and Jesus came back. There were angels and other people there. People were floating up to meet Him, then I stood up to join them, but I couldn't get off the ground. He turned around, and He left me. To top it off, my best friend Kaye told me that she had a dream that I went to hell. I was a mess! It was frightening. I was heartbroken. I felt that even Jesus had left me!

As children of divorce often do, I fantasized about Mom and Dad getting back together. That's not what happened. Mom remarried a man named Burt she met in a bar. She isn't even a drinker, but they shared their woes. He was a child molester. He didn't mess with me or with my sister, Kate, because we hated him enough. But he did abuse my sister, Katheryn. He messed up her life. When she was 12, she told my mother.

Katheryn was already drinking until she blacked out, and she was with a boy they didn't want her with, so they didn't

SURVIVING ABUSE AND ABORTION

believe her when she told them Burt abused her. Burt served jail time, but not for abusing Katheryn. He told me he didn't do it, and he even passed a lie detector test. Although Katheryn suffered greatly, the good news is that she is healthy and sober today. She is a miracle. She had chronic illness and weighed less than 90 pounds, but she prayed for God to help her, and He has. Finding out that my sister Katheryn was a victim of our stepfather was horrible for me. How could I not help her, save her? I was so wrapped up in myself, and I am still seeking healing from these thoughts and the feeling of responsibility.

When my baby sister Krista turned 18, Burt raped her at gunpoint. He served 30 consecutive weekends, and Mom finally divorced him. He since died a horrible death from cancer. Krista was calling out to Jesus during the rape. I asked her how she felt when Jesus didn't protect her, and she said, "Jesus was there, Bobbi, or I'd be dead." She has been in counseling, I'm sure, and she now has a beautiful, Christian home. She went to her pastor immediately, so she had support and love all around her.

Despite all that was going on at home, I enjoyed some very good times at an all-girls' high school. I made a lot of good girlfriends. We had boyfriends from the all-boys' high school. At 16, I fell in love. We had sex without any contraception, and I got pregnant. When I told my stepsisters about it, one of them said, "Have an abortion." Before that, I didn't even know about abortion, but I was scared, and I didn't want a baby. How selfish! My boyfriend took me to have the abortion. At the time, I told myself it was just a "blob of tissue," but deep down I knew better. I prayed for God's mercy! The way the vacuum felt on my uterus was awful. I swore to God I'd never do that again.

Then as a senior in high school, I became homecoming queen. Things were really going my way, at least at school. And I went and broke my promise to God. I was 17 when I realized I was pregnant again. I broke up with that boy and aborted his baby too. I decided I'd date lots of people, so I flirted around.

Then I met Rick. We got married at the courthouse. I barely knew my in-laws. I was out of church for 20 years. Then my son got sick, and I went back to church to beg God to heal him. Now, I love being a part of the body of believers; it is beautiful. Jesus "came back for me!"

Since the fall of man in the garden when Adam and Eve sinned, God made a way for me. If I was the only one on earth, He would do the same. It is what ultimately gives each of us value. Can you imagine perfect as God is perfect? We cannot. His idea of the perfect heaven includes us. Oh, my gosh! Sometimes it is so clear, obvious, and true. Other times it is like driving down a shady lane, but God is still there.

God will let us choose, though, and if we turn from him, He will let us go. We have free choice—a gift from Him. The best part of my life has happened in the last couple of years—my spiritual re-awakening. I know that I need God so much. I need to be in His lap at all times.

My best protection against the enemy is to be God's child. We come into the world with nothing, and everything we have is from Him. Just think, if He had not given us free will, then we would not have a way to give to Him. Even though it cost His son, He gave us a way. In the garden, before the soldiers came, He was sweating blood. He spoke, and they fell down!

SURVIVING ABUSE AND ABORTION

He didn't stay on the cross because He had to stay there. He did it for me.

—BOBBI STONE

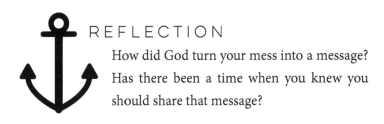

REFLECTION

How did God turn your mess into a message? Has there been a time when you knew you should share that message?

SURVIVING CAREGIVING

*"The godly people in the land are my true heroes!
I take pleasure in them."*

Psalm 16:3

I'll never forget June 6, 2012. My 18-year-old daughter and I were shopping in Franklin, Tennessee, enjoying the beautiful day. Some shopping days are meant for shopping, but other shopping days are meant for just being together. This day was for mother and daughter simply to be together. Since the weather was so nice, I thought walking in and out of shops on the town square would be fun, especially with a Starbucks nearby. There was one particular store I wanted to go in because I knew they would have a perfect gift for a friend of mine. She had just lost her husband a couple weeks earlier, and I had not yet bought her a gift just to let her know I was thinking of her.

As we pulled into the parking lot, my daughter looked at her cell phone and said, "Daddy is trying to call you." I pulled the car into Park and turned the engine off, then immediately called my husband. His first words were, "Mary Jo, have you talked to your mother?" I said, "No, why?" He said, "She's had an accident and they're taking her to the emergency room." This was such a strange thing to say to me. My mother? An accident?

You have to understand, my 73-year-old mother is amazing. She doesn't look her age, she's very intelligent, has tons of energy and for the past five plus years has been the sole caregiver for my 83-year-old daddy.

As I rushed back to the emergency room, I made eye contact with the first employee I saw. The lady said, "Go down the hall and to the left, the nurses will show you where she is." As I walked toward her, she looked up, saw me, and began to cry and repeat, "Honey, I'm so sorry." She knew, just as I knew, our lives and routine were about to change.

After the x-rays were taken, the doctor came to talk with us. They referred to the results as fractures and that the "fracture" in the right was worse than the left.

I asked the nurse point blank, "What do the x-rays really mean?"

"Well," she said, "both of your mother's legs are broken. Because osteoporosis is in both knees, the tibia bones broke into the knees and shattered them. These breaks are so bad we consider them trauma breaks, which require a specialized trauma doctor."

SURVIVING CAREGIVING

When I left the ER, I walked to the car, got in, and preceded to break down and cry. Now, I'm a pretty capable, independent woman, but at this moment, I felt like a helpless little girl. I remember crying out to God, "I'm so scared. Please help me! I don't know what to do with my daddy!"

My daddy...where do I start? Daddy was always the cut-up, picker, agitator, sociable, routine guy. He was retired from the post office, and everybody in town knew him. Over the past several years daddy had battled diabetes, heart by-pass surgery, a shunt in his head, Meniere's disease, and early stages of dementia. Yes, he could be negative and irritable at times, but by the grace of God, the silly humor remained intact.

The problem with all this was my mother was Daddy's caregiver. Now what would we do?

Thinking about the first couple of days of caring for Daddy is kind of fuzzy to me now. Yep, the answer to the question, "Who will take care of daddy?" was "ME!"

I do recall reading June 7th in my *Jesus Calling* devotional book. A portion of it read, "Who is in charge of your life? If it is you, then you have good reason to worry. But if it is I (Jesus), then worry is both unnecessary and counterproductive." Amazing how a devotional can so clearly speak to your circumstances. Over the next several months, this little devotional proved to line up so closely with my life, my emotions, and my unfamiliar journey.

When caring for an elderly parent, you tend to switch over to a moment mentality and just do what you need to do in that moment. I can't remember enough to describe in detail or in sequence, but I learned over the next 48 hours the needs of my daddy. I learned Daddy wore Depends with the big maxi pads in them. He called them "Pretends" instead, because he said you pretend you're peeing on your own. I learned that he used the urinal when he couldn't make it to the bathroom with the walker. So my mother had strategically placed urinals throughout the house—two in the bedroom and one in the laundry room. He could be watching TV and all of a sudden say, "Jo, I can't make it!" I'd run to the closest urinal, help him pull down his lounging pants and Depends and hope to catch the flow, which usually had already started. I came to appreciate those Depends and the brilliant person who created them.

I learned my daddy had a set schedule of eating and an extreme routine of meals. He had a huge breakfast, a huge lunch, and a light dinner. Daddy taught me his daily schedule, which was so exact that it would drive most crazy—the timing of his newspaper, the *Price is Right*, his shower, lunch, which lights you turn on and off throughout the day, dinner, putting on pajamas, turning on the nightlight in the bathroom, taking his hearing aid out, and getting in bed at exactly 9:00 p.m., with many more details in between. I wasn't sure if this was a man thing or when you get to be 83 years old, it is just comfort in a routine. How in the world did my mother do this for so many years? And how did she do it with a good attitude?

Mom has had her surgery and has been moved to the nursing home for rehabilitation. Three weeks have passed. I can't decide if they've passed quickly or slowly. Every other day, Daddy and I continue to go to the nursing home to see Mama. On days Daddy and I haven't gone to the nursing home, Mama and I talked on the phone, like we have every other day. We both are using *Jesus Calling* devotional, so we would encourage each other with it. If I am down, she encourages me; if she is down, I encourage her. Mama has made great progress with her legs. The physical therapists were amazed by this 73-year-old's determination and stamina.

The next transition was finding out that Mama would be coming home and completing her rehab there. The next big challenge for me was being a caregiver of two.

One of the decisions I made in my heart was when Mama came home was that she was in charge again! I had to remember this was her home, and I wanted her to feel like she called the shots and I served.

When Mama came home, we praised God! She was so excited, but I could tell she was nervous too. Within a month, Mama stood on both legs. Woo-hoo! She looked like a baby giraffe learning to walk. After a few days, she ditched the wheelchair and stuck with the walker. For four weeks, I continued my six-hour shift with weekends off. The caregivers continued to do a great job, but I knew it wouldn't be long until my mother would want everybody (including me) out of her house.

On November 9, 2012, Mama called and said they took Daddy to the emergency room. Come to find out, he had a host of things wrong with him, including her issues. As I stayed during the days at the hospital, I quickly realized Mama was definitely not up to par in her legs.

My brother and his wife came home at Christmastime and saw Daddy. They couldn't believe how much he had gone down.

Daddy lived at the nursing home for six months. Mama did

everything she could to make his room look homey. Physically, he couldn't walk anymore. Mentally, he also continued to decline.

My daddy turned 84 on May 21. On Tuesday, May 28, I met Mama at the nursing home for a regular visit. When it was time for Daddy's nap, she tucked him in, and we both kissed him bye. As always, he'd tell me, "I love you, Jo. I always look forward to seeing you".

On Wednesday, May 29, Mama went at her normal time to see Daddy. At 10:30 p.m. that night, the phone rang. She just knew it was the nursing home before she answered it. They said Mrs. Gunter, Mr. Gunter is being taken to the emergency room. Mama texted me I had better come on quickly. About ten miles from the hospital, my cell went off. I held my breath as I read the text from Mama—"He passed. I'll call your brother." It was 11:24 p.m.

The doctor said it was a hard heart attack, and that he went quickly. I walked over to him and touched his forehead. It was cold...a cold shell. Daddy was in heaven with all his friends. He was home and free.

Mama had asked me to do the eulogy, which I was honored to do. When it was my turn to speak, I took a deep breath and asked the Holy Spirit to be Lord over my words and gestures and emotions. I wanted this moment to bless my daddy's memory, to bless this room of special people, but most of all I wanted to please my Lord.

It has been a couple of months since Daddy passed. It's been over a year since Mama's accident. Time is a funny thing. It does go by so quickly. I've often thought about the lessons I

SURVIVING CAREGIVING

learned from taking care of Daddy and Mama. Most definitely, my faith grew and my compassion for other caregivers developed. God taught me more humility and how to persevere, and even when I feel like I'm exhausted and worn-out, there's always more I can give. Daddy taught me never go through a day without having a good laugh. He taught me always to let people know how much you appreciate them. Mama taught me how to never give up and keep moving forward. She taught me determination, discipline and endurance. Above all else, God taught me how to start trusting Him more. He's such a big God, and He's so aware of each of us. He promises in Hebrews 13:5 to never leave us, nor forsake us.

To all the caregivers out there who cook, clean, hold urinals, and do countless things I never even did, you are my heroes.

— MARY JO GRAHAM

 REFLECTION

Think of someone you know is hurting. Ask God to give you the strength to reach out to them in their time of need.

SURVIVING PUTTING CAREER FIRST

Yea, though I walk through the valley of the shadow of death, I will fear or dread no evil, for you are with me; Your rod and Your staff, they comfort me.

PSALM 23:4

My name is Kelly, and I'm a survivor. I am an only child who grew up in a small town in Oaklahoma. As a child, I always wanted to do everything right, was very sensitive, and got my feelings hurt easily. I was a people-pleaser from a very young age.

My dad was very strict, so I didn't have much of a relationship with him growing up, but I spent a lot of time with my mom. They were young parents, having gotten married at sixteen. Mom grew up with me and loved me unconditionally, so we were best friends. I was always trying to get Dad's approval and had a feeling that his love was conditional.

Dad was a songwriter, Mom was a singer, and I had aspirations of becoming a singer, so we moved to Nashville. Big dreams! After about eight years, my parents went through a bad divorce. I remember going back and forth between the two while they each went separate ways, trying to cope. I graduated from high school when mom went back to Oaklahoma for a while to be with her mother and to get her head straight.

I was dating my best friend from high school. He wanted to marry me, but I looked at him more as a friend. His parents wanted to take me in because I didn't really have a place to go, so I moved in with him and his family. That was a stupid choice; I just wanted a family. They were good people.

We eventually got married. He was my first sexual experience, and once I did that, I felt I had to marry him. We moved to Murfreesboro to go to school. Soon, he began to get abusive. As the abuse got worse—after about two years—he came to me and said the reason was so abusive to me was that he was bisexual. That was my ticket out. I stayed a few more months, but then I left him.

During this marriage, I had not spoken to my dad, but after the divorce, I began to start building back my relationship with him. I was actually working for him until he fired me after a fight about my mom. I immediately went back to non-communication with my dad.

Working as a bartender and still trying to get my music career off the ground, I dated a guy who wanted to marry me. At 22, I got pregnant and had an abortion without telling him

SURVIVING PUTTING CAREER FIRST

because I knew I didn't want to marry this guy. The only person I told was my best friend, who told me where to go and helped me with the money to do it. That was traumatic and affected me for many years. I didn't really work through the guilt of it until recently.

Next, I worked in a marketing department when I met and fell in love with a man named Kyle. We dated for six months, got engaged and married within a year. Kyle made me feel good, safe and truly loved. I dredged up the courage to tell him about my past. Instead of judging me, he accepted me, which made me love him more. I really felt Kyle would run when I told him about the abortion, but his loving acceptance increased my self-worth. We were married for nine years.

During this time, my relationship with Dad was as good as it could be, and he signed me to a record deal. As long as I did everything his way, we got along. But I eventually grew tired of doing everything his way, and Kyle wanted me to leave the record label. I tried to stay in the middle, because I didn't want my husband to get into conflict with Dad. I was guarded, afraid everything would blow up. I performed this balancing act for a long while, but finally decided to leave the label to please Kyle.

When I told Dad I wanted to leave the label and try new things, he took it as a personal attack, just as I had feared. I thought it would die down after a while, but a few weeks after I left, I got a horrible letter from Dad saying the most awful things a parent could say. He called me the "black sheep" of the family, said I was "bad seed," and many other things he made up in his head because he thought I wasn't loyal to him. I cried and cried, finally showing the letter to my husband. Kyle was shocked. I said I would never cry over him again.

When I shut off my feelings for my dad, I shut off all my feelings…except anger. I was angry at my husband, blaming him for wanting me to leave the label. I didn't say this to Kyle; I internalized my anger and shut away my other feelings inside. This continued for about two years. During this time, I stepped out of our marriage, after which, I really shut down, not wanting to face what I had done.

Maybe my dad had been right about me.

I had my first anxiety attack when I first told my husband I wanted a divorce. I told Kyle what I had done. He was very upset. I left, even though he wanted to forgive me and work it out. I just wanted to run away. Through all of this guilt, I had more violent anxiety attacks, crying uncontrollably, hyperventilating, etc. I went to a doctor who gave me anti-anxiety medication.

During all of this, I began to work on my relationship with God and became closer to Him. I was in Nashville, pursuing my music career and pouring my emotions into my writing. I had some suicidal thoughts, and all I knew to do was go to the Bible. I would open the Bible randomly and pray. Although I knew I didn't really want to kill myself, I had visions of doing it. As I walked past the knife rack, an image of grabbing one and quickly stabbing myself flashed in my mind. I know now that the devil was trying to win my soul, but constant prayer resulted in God helping me work through all of this. God began to reveal to me what He wanted me to be, and I was slowly becoming that.

At those times when I sought God through random Bible passages, God gave me peace. I read that I was created by God

SURVIVING PUTTING CAREER FIRST

as worthy. My grandmother's words came back to me: when you think you have nothing to be thankful for, look for the smallest things. When I woke up and the anxiety was on me, I'd think of the small things like my little dog Betsy licking my face. Little things and step by step I began to get better. As the realization sunk in that I am worthy, bitterness toward my dad fell away. It took two years, but the night I knew it was gone was the night I cried because I wanted Dad back in my life.

I emailed him later that night, he responded, and we had lunch the next day. Slowly, we began to rebuild our relationship. He never apologized, but I never expected him to. I have since taken what he's had to offer and let go of the rest. I'm thankful for that because he has now gone through cancer and a bone marrow transplant, and I've been able to be with him through all that.

After my divorce, I met a man through music. I thought he was great. We even wrote a song together. He is a Christian and is a humble, talented, good-looking guy. He wanted me to meet his parents, so we went to Montana. They were great people. I felt I was well, and this was my second chance. Looking back, I can see the signs were there, but I couldn't see them at the time.

He started using the skeletons in my closet to control me. I easily fell back into thinking I was not worthy and tried harder to please him. Soon, the situation became abusive. He wanted me to move to Montana and stay in music. I had not had an anxiety attack in a couple of years, but I had one when he continued to use my past against me. I hadn't realized how quickly I could fall back into that trap, but I just tried to please him more.

I continued to work on my relationship with Christ, by

reading the Bible, praying, and turning to God for help. Once again, He reminded me that I am worthy. When my fiancé's fighting got physical, I reached a turning point. He strangled me, threw something at me, and slammed me against the wall, and I pulled a knife on him to defend myself.

He left me alone for a while, then the fighting started again. I was bruised from being kicked, and my throat was sore from being strangled. I was scared about what he was capable of doing to me. At this point, my dad had cancer, so I told my fiancé I was leaving to return to Nashville to be with my dad and get my head straight. My fiancé was completely understanding until I let him know I wasn't coming back, then he got angry.

After I returned to Nashville, Mom told me that Kyle had called to ask about me. He had a dream about me and wanted to know if I was okay. I never told my mom about the abuse, but when I talked with Kyle, he told me he had dreamed I was being beaten by a man. I was amazed that we were this connected five years after our divorce. I had always held Kyle in my heart and had even prayed while I was in Montana that he would find a good Christian woman that would love him in a way he deserved. I never dreamed we could ever be together again. I had prayed, "God, if I'm not meant to be with Kyle, please take him out of my head." But He never did.

Back in Nashville, Kyle and I began to talk and date again. He had grown as an individual, which he said he needed to do. I had healed from many old wounds. God had not caused my abuse at the hands of my previous fiancé, but He was with me through it. I have learned to hear God's voice in all situations, making sure it lines up with His word in the scripture

SURVIVING PUTTING CAREER FIRST

and learning to recognize the lies of the enemy.

One way I felt the hand of God happened when I moved back and wanted to help women. It was soon after I began to date Kyle, and I was working on my jewelry business. A complete stranger asked, "Are you in the ministry?" I said no. She said, "You have a light about you, and I believe God has a lot in store for you this year. He is just loving on you right now." I felt it was God letting me know that I was headed in the right direction. What an affirmation!

Soon after that happened, I decided to start a ministry with my music, my jewelry, and my story of abuse. I started to write things down, and God reminded me of that woman in the store who affirmed me with a word from God. I learned that seeking success in my career above all else would never result in the peace that passes understanding.

I discovered that as I grew in my faith, God gave me peace and released me from the burden I had put on myself to be successful as a musician. I realized that my music did not define who He has designed me to be. Now, it was okay to just be me. He loves me, and I no longer have to perform.

And on June 22, 2014, Kyle and I were married again!

—Kelly Smith

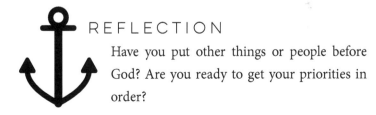

REFLECTION

Have you put other things or people before God? Are you ready to get your priorities in order?

SURVIVING CHRONIC PAIN

"I can do all things through Christ who strengthens me."

PHILIPPIANS 4:13

Growing up in Tulsa, Oklahoma, I was raised by a single mother, as my parents were divorced when I was two years old. My father was an alcoholic, and my mother was not much of a drinker. Mother worked more than one job at times to support us. When I was in ninth grade, she met another man. They dated through my high school years, and just before my graduation, they married and moved away. I moved in with my grandmother who then moved to Kansas to be with her husband at their second house. I proceeded to finish raising myself.

I was always a good girl, no drinking or drugs, and I was the designated driver. I had taken my first taste of alcohol and had experienced my first hangover at the age of 18 with my mother and stepdad. I realized I didn't like the taste and certainly did not like the aftereffects. My partying days were throughout my twenties with my friends with whom I did the sober "designated driving."

When I was twenty, I went to the lake in Oklahoma with a boy I was dating. After the day of his drinking beer and riding around the lake in the boat, we packed up to drive home. We were in my new car (the only new car I ever had), and we threw the empty beer cans in the truck, thinking we would dispose of the trash when we got home. As I was driving down the highway, a lady in another car did not see me behind a truck and she crossed over into our lane. We T-boned her, and I was thrown against the windshield, which I broke with my head. (I was not wearing a seatbelt, and since then am never without one.) The rearview mirror was broken either by my head or by something else. It went into my face and into my eye lobe. I hit the steering wheel so hard that I had rubber embedded in my chin. It, and glass, continued to come out of my skin as much as two years later. I bruised my chest so hard that I had to wear a heart monitor for two days afterwards. My knees were severely bruised against the steering column.

I don't remember anything much except that I did come to shortly after impact, and a nice gentleman was beside me asking if I was okay. All I said was, "Are all my teeth okay?" He said, "Honey, I can't see them for all the blood." I replied, "Please grab something and check." I said my mom had spent

SURVIVING CHRONIC PAIN

$1200 on my teeth, and she would shoot me if I had broken them. He grabbed a shirt out of my bag and checked to see that my teeth were okay, and they were. I passed out again, and the next thing I remember was waking up in a Tulsa hospital. A doctor's finger was through the hole in my chin as he was cleaning it out. I screamed, and he told me to hush because there were other people in the hospital.

After the accident, I found out the woman in the other car was at fault and was drinking. I also discovered that the guy I was with got me in trouble because he was drinking. When I looked in my purse, I had no driver's license and had been given a ticket for "open container." I knew I did not drink, so after it was over I was able to get a copy of the hospital's blood test to prove I had no alcohol in my system. Then I got my license back. An attorney contacted me, and we sued the other driver. Also, the guy I was with sued me for negligence and sued the other lady. Needless to say, we stopped dating at that point.

When I woke up from the accident, I had the most horrendous headache I'd ever had due to the concussion. I had dislocated my jaw and my nose was swollen until it was huge. I had always had difficulty swallowing medicine, even as a small child, so from this point on I was on something intravenously. I remember thinking *what will I do after the hospital for this pain because I cannot swallow medicine?*

This began twenty-eight years of chronic pain and headaches, which I received relief from during my two pregnancies. I had no pain when I was pregnant, but one cannot stay pregnant for years, so the pain returned. The long road ahead was one of many, many attempts at pain medications, diets, therapies, etc. I tried everything you can imagine to get rid of the pain, including many types of doctors who all thought they could fix me. I went to every therapist you can imagine, even a cranial massage therapist. Sometimes I would get maybe 24 hours of relief, but the headaches would always, always, always come back.

My children suffered immensely because they knew I had to have quiet around me. My ex-husband could irritate me by turning on lights, which aggravated my pain. He got mad because I was in bed. So, it killed my first marriage because I was in bed every weekend. He was an outdoor person, and I couldn't be outdoors in the bright sun. I had to give up the outdoors, loud movies, and concerts during those years. I missed a lot of life. It makes me so sad to think about it now. My kids missed a lot too.

I've lost count of how many different pain meds I have tried over the years. When my friends would have some pain issue, I'd ask if I could try their medication to see if it would help me. Because I was always desperate to be pain-free, I would often leave a note on my bedside table so that if anything happened my friends would know everything I had in my system. My doctor had told me that pain and the results of the accident would mess with my memory, so I definitely had memory issues.

Luckily, I never lived alone. I always had my children, and I knew that if something happened they would call someone. But when you are in that much pain, you get desperate for anything that will give you relief. If someone had said that standing on your head in manure would get rid of the pain I would have said, "Okay, where is the manure?" I even tried smoking marijuana. For about two years, a friend begged me to try it. So finally I did, and of course, it did not work. It just made me paranoid. I was glad it didn't because I did not like that feeling, and more importantly, it is not legal.

My mother moved here 2 ½ years ago after we had been apart for many years. She had not been around so she really had no idea how bad it was for me. Of course, she wanted to do fun things on the weekends. She did not know that I had not been able to shop, go out or do anything outdoors for years. Finally, she said, "We must do something about this. It's ridiculous!" She called my cousin to tell her how bad off I was and talked to my cousin's husband, whom I'd met at their wedding in my 20s. He was then studying to be a pain management doctor and is now one of the world's leading in this field. I had never wanted to bother my family. I knew he was a busy doctor, and I did not want to call upon him.

My mother called my aunt who called him, and he asked me to call him. It's not that I didn't want a cure, but I was embarrassed as to how bad off I was and felt like I was "using" my family. Regardless, he got on the stick and found me a doctor in Franklin, Tennessee, and they had an appointment immediately. This pain specialist at the time was the only one in our area doing this work. He saw me. I took him a letter outlining everything I had been through and everything I had tried. First, a new patient has to attend a seminar. I listened to everything he had to say and right away said, "Where do I sign up?" The doctor said I was the perfect candidate, so we did a trial for this procedure. It is called a cranial neurostimulator implant. The trial consisted of wires that went into the back of my neck and to a box that I could control. This was for 5-7 days just to see if it would work for me.

The trial required a two-hour surgery, then we were to wait two days to put the wires in place. During this procedure, I don't know if they "messed with" some nerves or what, but when I came out of the anesthesia, I felt better immediately. It was bizarre. After the surgery, Mom and I went out to eat and I felt like a new person. I felt so good and the stimulator wasn't even on yet. I had planned to go home to rest, and I couldn't sit down! I felt they had touched upon something miraculous. Then a couple days later, I went back for them to turn on the stimulator. I still felt good. That weekend, Mom, Trevor and I went to a street fair where I could be in the sun. There was loud music, and it didn't hurt! I was feeling so wonderful after walking all over the place.

When my week was up, I went back to the doctor and they hooked up the device. He asked me what was the improvement I'd experienced, and I told him absolutely 100 percent! We then started the paperwork to get the permanent implant done. That took some doing, and they turned me down twice, but then they relented. They had turned us down for the trial and for the permanent procedure, but they finally gave in.

Then something really weird happened. Mom and I had planned a trip to Italy. I started to feel bad again, but we went on the trip, and on the way home, something happened on that plane. When I got off the plane at home I didn't have any headaches. We never figured it out, but it was too good to be true.

SURVIVING CHRONIC PAIN

On my 48th birthday, the headaches came back and they came back with a vengeance. I immediately called Dr. Rupert and asked, "When can we get the permanent implant scheduled." It couldn't be soon enough for me. It took some back and forth with insurance, but it was done on October 17. It was the worse surgery ever. It took four to five hours. Leads (wires) are run from and through your back up through the shoulders to the head then around each side of your forehead. They had difficulty bringing me out of the anesthesia so it was dark when we went home. Mom took me home, and my friends were there waiting for me. I got out of the car and became very sick, throwing up all over everyone's feet including my own. I hurt so bad, I cried, "What have I done?" My husband called my Mom, and everyone was so worried. The next day, I felt some better. Then, we went back to have permanent implant turned on.

Now, after some time of learning how to adjust/set the stimulator at the correct level, and after one and a half years, I have my life back. The headaches do come back but now I can control them with Excedrin and the stimulator. I'm amazed at how I can get work done at my job. It's like I'm a dynamo! I can do my job and help others. I can exercise now, walk, and ride my bike. I started back to my kickboxing class and other things I haven't been able to do before.

Those who have them know that the word "headache" does not even begin to describe a migraine. Chronic migraine never goes away, always there waiting for the right moment to ruin your day. Many people turn against God and say "Why?" or "Why me?" I am glad that I can say I never once blamed God. I've been in church since I was a baby. My faith has always been there. I knew there was a reason for going through this—at some point, I will be able to help someone else. I felt that I would eventually be able to tell others what I had experienced and would be able to give them hope. My mother has also met people who experience chronic pain. One person became a really good friend to me and she is having this surgery soon. I can say to people, "Don't give up." There is a reason for everything and God has said he will never leave me and He has not. I have two boys to raise and I always felt that someday I would get relief and that God would see me through to that day.

There are people all over the world who are benefiting from this surgery and I am so grateful to God for providing it for me.

—Michele Bufford

REFLECTION

Have you ever blamed God for something? What do you believe He wanted you to learn from this experience?

SURVIVING WAITING FOR MR. RIGHT

My soul finds rest in God alone;
my salvation comes from him.
He alone is my rock and my salvation;
He is my fortress, I will never be shaken.

PSALM 62:1–2

From my earliest memories, I knew I wanted to be a missionary, a wife, and a mother. When I was a blond-haired, blue-eyed princess, my favorite games were playing mommy and teacher. Just like many other Southern girls, I picked up cultural expectations and wore them proudly. But as I matured, it became evident that the traditional approach to love and dating was not going to work for me. What appeared to be the socially acceptable norm was not what God was calling me to be, so I stumbled around with little guidance trying to meet a higher standard.

When I graduated from high school, I just knew that I would find a godly husband at a Christian college, so I set off for Lee University like a girl in pursuit of the perfect pair of shoes. Fortunately, God knew the weaknesses in my heart, and in His grace and mercy, He protected me from myself and placed a prayer in my heart.

During my freshman year, having seen through others' experiences the pitfalls of making my life about a guy, I pleaded with the Lord. In a moment that could only have taken place through His grace and mercy, I begged God, "Do not bring me a husband until I know you are all I need." Little did I know at the time what I was asking!

Throughout college, I stumbled over my own desires, experienced a few heartbreaks, and sought direction from several recommended authors. I read *What to Do While You are Waiting*, *Lady in Waiting*, *Passion & Purity*, and *Boy Meets Girl*. I attended the New Attitude conference by Joshua Harris and Sovereign Grace Ministries. Despite my best efforts, I remained frustrated that I could not seem to do what everyone advised—find contentment. "Until you are content, God will not bring you your mate," they said. And ever-present was the whispered prayer, "God, don't bring me a husband until I know You're all I need."

Despite my aspirations of contentment, being single became my thorn in the flesh as I wore one bridesmaid's dress after another. Graduation came and went, and I realized that

SURVIVING WAITING FOR MR. RIGHT

life was not turning out the way I had imagined. Even though I had done all the things a "good Christian girl" is supposed to do, I had still not found "the one."

At this point, a terrible war erupted in and for my very soul. My flesh fought against the Spirit within me, battling for my salvation. I had been raised in a Christian home and accepted Jesus into my heart as a humble and innocent child with the limited understanding of a child. However, as I passed through childhood and sailed past adolescence and into young adulthood, I had never fully realized my need for a Savior. What had passed for Christianity up until this point no longer met my needs. The desire for a husband began to consume me and threw me into the pits of despair. I wondered why I couldn't muster up the strength to get over this.

One day on my way to visit one of my dear married friends, God in His infinite mercy met me in one of my darkest moments, and He showed me something that changed my life. It was this: when I realized that I was incapable of saving myself, of overcoming these issues in my life, this was the realization I thought I had committed to before—that He is all I need. In that moment, I found my Savior, and I ceased my laboring, coming into a place of sweet rest that I had never known.

While I rejoiced in my newfound strength and renewed commitment to contentment, my struggle once more reared its ugly head. My best friend became the last of our friends to marry, and the unthinkable happened; my younger brother found love and married before me. I spent countless hours being discontent about being discontent! I knew I had a loving Savior who could supply all my needs. What more could I possibly want? Why couldn't I just be happy? What was wrong with me?

Eventually, my mother said something profound in a way that only a mother can say. "Miki," she advised, "you must become content about your discontentedness." At first, this sounded crazy to me. Then I began to ask myself the question, What does it mean to be content? Could it be that contentedness was not the blissful feeling that bluebirds were encircling my head and flowers were blooming around my feet? When I went to the scriptures to see what He had to say about it, I discovered it meant otherwise. Paul said in Philippians 4:11–13 (KJV):

> "Not that I speak in respect of want: for I have learned in whatsoever state I am, therewith to be content. I know both how to be abased, and I know how to abound: every where and in all things I am instructed both to be full and to be hungry, both to abound and to suffer need. I can do all things through Christ which strengtheneth me."

Paul *learned* to be content, whatever his circumstances. That means that Paul had run the gamut of conditions and situations to bring him to an understanding and stance of total contentment. So, then, what exactly *does* it mean to be content? The *Encarta Dictionary* defines *content* as being "quietly satisfied and happy" and to "accept or make do with something." Paul had learned to desire no more than what he had, and he was ready and willing to accept God's will for his life.

SURVIVING WAITING FOR MR. RIGHT

Contentment is complete happiness about my current "single" status, thinking I could conquer the world in a single bound of single-womanpower!

Contentment, simply put, is faith. It takes faith to be ready to accept and willing for what God has for your life. It's a total reliance on God to make that happen and to work *all* things for my good. I may not be joyfully exuberant about being single, but I'll be desiring God above a husband and willingly accepting His sovereign will for my life.

When I came to this realization, it made contentment seem like a possible state of mind. I could believe in God's faithfulness in my weakness. This message is for the humble. It is for those of us who say, "My life does not look like what I had imagined. My perfectly laid plans have failed; but I know and love, trust and serve a Savior who cares for me and knows my needs. I trust that Savior with whatever He chooses to bring into my life, and no matter what He does, He is good, faithful, and trustworthy."

I want to quit laboring in my own strength and fling myself on Him in abandon and say, "I am content in You for You are all I need!" This is how Paul could conclude, "Most gladly therefore will I rather glory in my infirmities, that the power of Christ may rest upon me. Therefore I take pleasure in infirmities, in reproaches, in necessities, in persecutions, in distresses for Christ's sake: for when I am weak, then am I strong." (2 Corinthians 12:9–10 KJV)

Our ultimate joy is not found in everything working out according to our plans, but in the life of Jesus being revealed in our hearts. A beautiful wedding may be desirable, but being a beautiful Bride of Christ is so much more! My wedding day will be one of celebration and joy, blessed by God. That blessing, in whatever form it comes, is what my heart longs for more than anything.

— Miki Creasman

REFLECTION

Name some things that bring joy to your soul.

SURVIVING DIVORCE

My grace is sufficient for you.
My strength is made perfect in your weakness.

2 CORINTHIANS 12:9

I never imagined that I would be a divorcée. I grew up in a very loving family. We were extremely close. My parents were married for 36 years. Their marriage ended when my dad died of lung cancer at age 62. I always felt secure that my parents loved me. They were very supportive. I remember my dad would always say, "If you're going to be a ditch digger, be a great ditch digger!" He believed in doing 100 percent.

I am the youngest of four. My dad was in the military police. I was upset when my dad retired because that meant we would no longer be traveling, and I loved to travel. I had so many friends. I didn't feel robbed of my childhood. I always liked school. My parents couldn't afford for me to go to a big college, so I went to a junior college.

I always thought I would be a missionary when I grew up. My mom and I prayed for my dad who was not a Christian, and he received Christ as his Savior about six years before he passed away! Yay, God!

I was taught to be very independent. My hobbies have always been sewing and cross-stitching. My first job was in a nursing home at age 16. I loved taking care of people. I knew I wanted to be in the nursing profession.

I met my first husband in nursing school. Tom and I dated for two years. He seemed to be a great guy. He was certainly exciting. We went camping and hiking. He was real. When we dated, the Christian thing didn't really enter my mind. We did start going to church, and he did accept the Lord.

The thing that happened to this marriage is something that love blinders don't let you see. He was incredibly selfish. We had periods of serving the Lord, then periods of not serving Him. Tom was from divorced parents, and he was always looking for inner peace, but would not allow God to give it to him.

I plunged heavily into serving the Lord, and Tom decided that he would go the other way! He met a person who he worked with. They both started doing cocaine, which led to an affair. He continued this secret life for about five years.

We tried Christian counseling for a while, and it became evident that he wanted me to be medicated. I was angry with Tom and with God. I felt like God should not have let that happen to me. I had been serving Him.

Tom was never committed to working on our marriage. I was trying to deal with the situation. He was never open and honest with me, so we swept it under the rug.

One year later, he started back up with everything again. I was a little bit wiser to his games.

I began to pray for God to deliver me from this situation. I went on a mission trip to the Amazon, and when I came back, it was over.

We divorced after 19 years. I was single again.

I spent time traveling around, working at different hospitals. I was so angry as a result of all of these things that happened. I started working on getting better by exercising and surrounding myself with friends and family.

Since I wasn't getting any flowers myself, I started giving flowers to others. Mostly, I stayed busy trying to keep my mind off of things. After two years, I went back to church. I stopped being angry with God, once I figured out he was protecting me all the time!

I finally went to see my mom. I knew she was so disappointed and burdened by all that had happened.

One of the most difficult challenges of being single was not having someone to share special moments. I was fine being by myself, with God and my three cats, of course! I was happy enjoying my peace.

I had a girlfriend who kept saying she had a friend in Tennessee she wanted me to meet. I was living in South Georgia. She set me up with a blind date with Don. Little did I know, he had been praying for a wife!

We talked on the phone for hours. We both had been on the same medical mission trip a year apart. We decided to meet at the Cracker Barrel because I felt it was safe. My girlfriend and I had this joke about what kind of a man I wanted God to give me. I wanted a 6-foot tall man who had a good sense of humor. Don is a 5'8", bald, fit guy! But I had decided I was going to see what the Lord had in store for me.

We have our own ideas about what is best for us. Don made me feel special. He was genuine. He asked me to go to Israel. After six months, he proposed, and we got married on September 30 at World Outreach Church.

There are three bits of advice I would give to a single person:

1. Don't beat yourself up over the divorce.
2. Control your anger.
3. There is no shame in seeing a Christian counselor.

I would also recommend the book, *What's so Amazing about Grace?* by Philip Yancey. The message given in this book has been a rich blessing to me.

Three things I will never do:

1. I will never understand or underestimate God's grace and mercy.
2. I will never underestimate the lengths that people will go to when God is in charge.
3. I will never be ungrateful for the blessing of a faithful, loving family.

SURVIVING DIVORCE

Taking responsibility for my part in each of my relationships, trusting those who love me, and letting God be God help me continue to heal. For those who are walking this same path, it will work for you too.

— Olphelia Langford

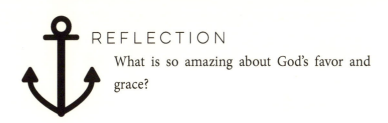

REFLECTION
What is so amazing about God's favor and grace?

SURVIVING THE NIGHTMARE BOSS

*Put on the whole armor of God that you may be able
to stand against the strategies and deceits of the devil.
For we wrestle not against flesh and blood,
but against principalities, powers,
against the rulers of the darkness of this age,
against spiritual hosts of wickedness in the heavenly places.*

Ephesians 6:11–12

In August 2008, just a few months into my new job, I got a new boss. Things started out fine, but within months of getting to know him, he became a Dr. Jekyll and Mr. Hyde. My office mates and I began to see things that disturbed us. We watched as he started with what I will call his first victim. Beginning with harassing them, he went on to threaten their job and made their life miserable.

Things got so bad that our group could tell what kind of mood he was in by the way he pulled up the blinds in his office. If they came up hard and fast, you didn't dare speak to him. If they came up slowly, he was approachable, but at your own risk, of course. We tried to avoid him if at all possible, but nothing seemed to work.

In Spring 2011, it was my turn, and over the following year, he made my life nearly unbearable. Sometimes I worked all night to make sure my projects and day-to-day tasks were perfect so he wouldn't have anything to complain about. But no matter how well I performed, it wasn't good enough. He told me it wasn't how he wanted it done or how he would have approached it.

Now, I have been a single parent since my 26-year-old son was 2. If I needed to work two jobs to make sure we had a roof over our heads and food on the table, then that's what I did. Rather than crying or becoming paralyzed, I tend to be a "put on your big girl pants," do what you need to do, and move on kind of person. But the constant harassment became more than I could handle, especially since I wasn't letting on to my family how bad things really were. They knew he was pushing my buttons, but I slowly felt paralyzed.

One late November night just before Thanksgiving, I was lying in bed and started crying uncontrollably. I had allowed myself to be pushed to the point that I felt I had nowhere to turn.

God had other ideas.

He used a couple of ladies with whom I was doing a home

SURVIVING THE NIGHTMARE BOSS

Bible study to show me that He had a greater plan for me. As Bible study was winding down one night, I asked the ladies if they had any words of wisdom about my situation because I was at my wits' end.

One of the ladies told me about being in a similar situation. She said that she would come home every day and complain to her husband about her boss. He got tired of hearing about it and told her to quit her job, but instead of quitting, she decided to seek God—study His Word and ask Him to show her how to deal with the person. That night, she shared these verses with me.

Servants, do what you're told by your earthly masters. And don't just do the minimum that will get you by. Do your best. Work from the heart for your real Master, for God, confident that you'll be paid in full when you come into your inheritance. Keep in mind always that the ultimate Master you're serving is Christ. The sullen servant who does shoddy work will be held responsible. Being a follower of Jesus doesn't cover up bad work. (Colossians 3:22-25)

What I'm getting at, friends, is that you should simply keep on doing what you've done from the beginning. When I was living among you, you lived in responsive obedience. Now that I'm separated from you, keep it up. Better yet, redouble your efforts. Be energetic in your life of salvation, reverent and sensitive before God. That energy is *God's* energy, energy deep within you, God himself willing and working at what will give him the most pleasure. Do everything readily and cheerfully—no bickering, no second-guessing allowed! Go out into the world uncorrupted, a breath of fresh air in this squalid and polluted society. Provide people with a glimpse of good living and of the living God. Carry the light-giving Message into the night so I'll have good cause to be proud of you on the day that Christ returns. You'll be living proof that I didn't go to all this work for nothing. (Philippians 2:12–16)

Through her Bible study and prayer, she discovered that if she served her boss as if she were serving Jesus Christ Himself then she was acting with the love and grace Jesus would show each of us. I began to study these scriptures and prayed for God's guidance. After some time, I decided to find a way to serve my boss as if I were serving Jesus.

Webster's New Collegiate Dictionary defines *study* as "application of the mental faculties to the acquisition of knowledge" and "a state of contemplation or reverie." Study is an adventure—the doorway to discovery. Through study, we transcend narrow and superficial understanding and begin to see more deeply into reality. It means learning to love God with your mind.

After I decided to begin studying those scriptures and seeking God's guidance, I found time to do a daily devotion using a daily devotional book. Two of the books I used were *Jesus Calling* by Sarah Young and *The Upper Room* (upperroom.com). The scriptures I read came from *The Message*, a paraphrased version of the Bible. I chose *The Message* because it is easier for me to understand. You can go to Biblegateway.com and pick any version of the Bible. The most important thing is that you find a version that you feel comfortable reading.

Finding a time for my devotional reading was difficult, but since I felt the need for God's guidance every morning before

SURVIVING THE NIGHTMARE BOSS

I walked into that office, I got to work early and sat in my car for about 20 minutes, reading from my devotional book and studying the scriptures using the acronym SOAP.

> **S** is for Scripture – I wrote out the passage from the Bible and read it out loud.
> **O** is for Observation – I wrote about what I got out of the passage in my journal.
> **A** is for Application – I thought about how I could apply this passage to my day.
> **P** is for Prayer – I asked God how I could use the verses to serve my boss that day.

As I practiced this approach, I began to notice small changes in how my office mates treated each other. Even I was affected. This example is pretty small, but when someone sneezed, I said, "Bless you." At first, others looked at me like I had three heads. But as I continued doing small things like this, others began to talk about God in my presence.

One day, a lady from another department caught me at the copier and asked if we could speak privately. We went into a conference room and shut the door. She told me about some serious medical issue she was facing and asked me to pray for her. I was so stunned that at first I didn't realize that she meant for me to pray for her then and there. So I did, and I realized that God was working all around me.

This lady did not grow up going to church or around Christian people. She had never really read the Bible. I invited her to a Presbyterian women's conference where I found out that she had never owned a Bible. After the conference, I gave her a Bible, and now she reads and studies her Bible every day.

By choosing to serve my boss as if I were serving Jesus I found that I was studying my Bible more each day. I was learning from my study that by serving this man this way, I was growing a relationship with my boss and, more importantly, with Jesus. I noticed that instead of throwing invoices at me, my boss would place them in my chair or my inbox. His tone of voice softened as did mine and my office mates. After months of Bible study and prayer, my boss's harshness began to melt away.

My boss retired in October 2012. In early 2013, I found myself fighting breast cancer. This man who had been such a tyrant—the one I had allowed myself to be paralyzed by for close to a year—called to let me know he was praying for me and to wish me well. He told me about a Bible study that he and a friend were starting at his church. It would be geared toward single parents and those going through divorce.

What I had seen as an impossible situation was simply a chance for me to grow closer to God and put my faith into practice. God can use anything and anyone to draw His children to His side—even a nightmare boss.

— KAY CROMWELL

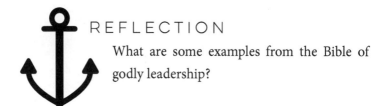

REFLECTION

What are some examples from the Bible of godly leadership?

SURVIVING CO-DEPENDENCY

Yet I am confident I will see the Lord's
goodness while I am here in the land of the living.
Wait patiently for the Lord. Be brave and courageous.
Yes, wait patiently for the Lord.

PSALM 27:13–14

I was born the middle child of three siblings. We were reared in a very small town. The train ran right down the middle of the town. I lived most of my time with my grandfather because my father was a working, functioning alcoholic. He spent much time hanging out in beer joints. There was lots of anger and tension in our home.

When I was four years old, my brother sexually abused me.

He would bring friends over to the house, and I was the entertainment. I suppressed these memories for a number of years. I was angry at my father who was not treating my mother well, and I was angry at the brother who was supposed to be taking care of me. Somehow, even as a child, I knew not to tell. I kept this secret all to myself until now. To this day, I have never talked to my brother about what he did to me.

In school, I turned to studying. It was an escape for me because studying wasn't emotional. My plan was to excel so that I could go to college.

In college, I didn't have a boyfriend until I was 21, and I ended up marrying him. We were married for five years. Within 36 months, I had three children and a husband who was cheating on me. I learned that he and I were in love with the same person—he loved himself, and I loved him too! When he left, I had two in diapers, and the oldest was four. Believe it or not, it really was a relief to be single.

At this time, I never thought of going to a counselor. I thought it would be better to talk to my preacher. He would give me scripture, but you could tell he did not have experience with helping divorced people.

Even though my experiences with men had been bad ones, I had not given up all of them. I began dating a guy named Bart. He seemed stable and very smart. Just what I was looking for. The first week we went out, he wanted to go to church with us. I didn't ask God, but I just knew this had to be from the Lord. Everything was going so smoothly, but some part of me knew there was a problem there.

Bart made me feel secure. He was good with my boys,

always home, and never angry. Bart adopted the boys, and he was a good father to them. Bart was going to school, working, and trying to get a promotion. During this time, I found out that he was deeply troubled.

Bart told me he was hearing voices. I asked him to go to the doctor. He was so scared because he had never experienced anything like this before. Bart went to a counselor who recommended that he take six Valium pills a day. The medication really put him "out there." It really began to get scary.

I found a counselor for myself and told him what was going on. He gave me a book on co-dependency. He said it was not healthy to have no concern for myself. I got the book *Co-dependent No More*, and for the first time, I saw myself as a caretaker of everyone.

I began to realize I was in a dangerous situation. Bart had tried to choke me. I was in the bathroom, and when I saw his face in the mirror, he had a scary look in his eyes.

Bart and I finally separated. He contacted me and threatened suicide if I didn't give him a divorce. Somehow, in my spirit I knew he was serious. I was at work, and I tried to think of a place Bart might go. I left and went to his grandfather's farm, and there he sat with a gun in his hand. He pointed it at me and said, "Do you want me to shoot your brains out or mine?" It was as if time stood still.

We divorced, and I felt safe.

His first suicide attempt was about five months later. With mental illness, you can be fine one day and lose it the next. Bart left us and never came back. He committed suicide one year later.

The boys and I never quit going to church. I knew the only way I could get through each day was with God.

It has been sixteen years since I've had a serious relationship. I can look back and see what my efforts got me, so I don't want to try to find myself another man. I am waiting and trusting God for what he has for me. I don't think he needs the service of match.com or eHarmony! At this time in my life, God is allowing me to be single and satisfied.

—SARAH BETH JONES

REFLECTION

Why does God allow times of difficulty and darkness? How does God help as I wait upon Him?

SURVIVING THE LOSS OF CHILDREN

I must calm down and turn to God, only he can rescue me.
He is my rock, the only one who can save me.
He is my place of safety, where no army can defeat me.

PSALMS 62:1-2

In the fall of 2009, my husband Wayne and I were preparing for a new chapter in our lives: becoming empty nesters. Boy, did *that* not happen!

On Thursday, October 8, 2009, around 3:00 p.m., our daughter-in-law Barbara came into the house as she did every day to pick up her son Isaiah. On this day, she had a gentleman with her, and he was wearing an EMS uniform. Our beautiful young daughter Jessica—a new bride and mother of a two-year-old daughter and a three-week-old son, preparing to leave for Montana on the upcoming Monday—had been killed in an accident.

Over the next several days, family and friends gathered around us as we prepared to bury our daughter and sort out the details. I went into survival mode overnight, going from being a grandmother to being the primary caregiver to a 2-year-old child.

I sought refuge in the Word of God. Without it, I would have lost my mind. During this time, I also went through grief counseling. My children and my husband had always been my life.

On Saturday, September 4, 2010, around 4:27 a.m., exactly 11 months since Jessica's accident, we received a call from our daughter-in-law, Brandy's, mother Michelle. She was in Florida visiting our son, Jonathan, and Brandy and helping with their seven-week-old daughter Madison. Upon waking, Brandy had found Jonathan unresponsive in the bathroom.

At first, I thought, *She can't be saying what I think she's saying. Have I lost another child? My God, this can't be.* At that moment, the Lord swooped Wayne and me up in His arms, and He's been carrying us ever since.

Losing two children in eleven months should have made me crazy, but it was five years in October, and our Lord has turned tragedy into triumph. We are living a new normal. I have gained sons and daughters that I didn't birth but are connected by heart. The process has been the hardest I have ever been through, but I live victorious knowing that our Savior is my rock, my refuge and the lifter of my head.

SURVIVING THE LOSS OF CHILDREN

We started with three children, and now only our firstborn son is left. God had great plans for this young man. Jason Duane Scales is not only my only child and my friend, but he is now my pastor also. I get to encourage him, but as my pastor, he gets to comfort and encourage me along with our entire membership as well as our community. All I can say is God is good, He is in control, and I trust Him completely.

—SHELIA SCALES

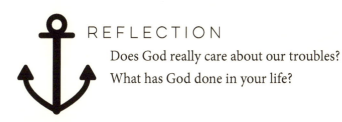

REFLECTION

Does God really care about our troubles?
What has God done in your life?

SURVIVING POWERLESSNESS

He gives strength to the weary and to him who lacks might He increases power.

ISAIAH 40:29

My husband had an affair. We divorced, and my son went with his father. It was over a year and a half before he came to see me. At the end of the visit, my son's daddy refused to take him back. I think it was because he was tired of taking care of his son.

I remarried in 2001 to my current husband who had colon cancer in 1998. In 2002, the cancer came back in his left lung. He lost part of his lung in surgery, and while he was in the hospital, his mother had a massive heart attack and died. He came home for her funeral, and the next day, he packed up, moved out and divorced me on April 1. He said he did not want me to go through what he knew was coming in his cancer fight. I reassured him, and we remarried on April 20.

In 2003, a four-inch brain tumor was discovered in my husband, and he had surgery again. He had 16 radiation treatments and chemotherapy from March to September. By October, he had another brain tumor in the same spot. The week of Thanksgiving, he had surgery again. He came home on Thanksgiving Day, but I took him back to the hospital the day after. He was basically in a coma with an infection on the brain.

After three and a half weeks, they told me he would never come home. He was only breathing six times a minute. His daughters and I got in his face and told him it was okay. Within a few minutes, he was awake and breathing normally. He wasn't ready to go. I took him home in December and promised that I would care for him as long as he lived and that I wouldn't put him in a nursing home. In July, he went back to the hospital, then to Alive Hospice where he died on July 28, 2004.

On July 26 that year, my mother had been to the doctor and had to have surgery for colon cancer. I cried out to God and told him I could not do this again. That was two and a half years ago, and Mama just turned 81. She never had treatments, and she has been cancer-free since 2004. God answered my prayers for her and for my own relief.

During my husband's illness, I had damaged my neck lifting him. In 1999, I had my first neck fusion. In 2008, I had the second neck fusion and was experiencing paralysis up and down my side and back. In April 2011, I had a third neck fusion. C3, 4, 5, 6, and 7 are fused with titanium screws. This surgery par-

SURVIVING POWERLESSNESS

alyzed my vocal cords, so I had surgery again in June. I had ear surgery in July of that year for chronic ear problems.

In April 2012, I had back surgery to insert rods and screws because of a congenital issue. In August, I went to my gynecologist and got the devastating, embarrassing news that I had the HPV virus. The doctor removed all he could, and he told me that I was in the last stages before invasive cancer. In researching the subject, I found that cervical cancer is almost always caused by this virus and that it can lie dormant for years. Because of the stage I was in, we knew it had been there a long time. In August 2013, this surgery had to be done again because of a recurrence of the virus.

I have been through a lot. I've been put to sleep a lot. I cannot tell you how many MRIs, scans, and other tests I've had. Through this journey, I asked God if I was a bad person. People tell me they think I am very strong. I think, *If only they knew.* But I know that all of this has made me who I am today. It forced me to see what I am made of, and part of that is faith. Through all my trials and tribulations, I never felt God left me alone. I know that without Him, I never would have made it this far. I have prayed continually that He would help me get through things and that He would help me be strong.

Now, once again, I'm called to be a survivor. Mother is still with me. She is showing signs of dementia. She has always been my best friend, and she and I are having some difficulties with this. She also has back problems, but surgery is not an option because of her age. I try to take care of her to the best of my ability. At the same time, she is trying so hard not to give up what independence she has left, so we struggle.

During all I have been through, there have been days when I could barely get out of bed. I wanted to give up. At times, I said, "I can't do this," but I did. Despite taking a lot of medication, I am still in pain. Sometimes I think I want to get into my car and go until I can't get back. It is just too hard. But with God, all things are possible. Never give up or blame God. Keep Him in your heart. He won't give us more than we can bear. In fact, he blesses us beyond measure. I focus on the fact that I have two wonderful children who have never given me any trouble. One is an ordained minister. I have much to be thankful for.

— Tonya Smithson

REFLECTION

Why is it important to have a thankful heart? How can I praise, worship and express my thankfulness to God today?

LOOKING FOR ANSWERS WHILE IN THE STORM?

Why?

Why am I going through this?

Why am I here?

Who am I?

These questions have intrigued people forever. The answers can only be discovered by understanding God's plan for you and by getting to know Jesus Christ.

Who is Jesus? What Did He Do?

Jesus Christ, the Son of God, came into the world as a human being, lived a sinless life, died on the cross and rose from the dead to save humanity from dying in their sins.

Christ died to pay for our sins so your sins can be forgiven. And because Jesus conquered death, you can have eternal life.

But this gift of forgiveness and eternal life cannot be yours unless you...

Ask for forgiveness

Believe in the gift of salvation

Pray to confess your sin

Receive Christ into your life

Scriptures to Help You in Your New Life

John 3:16, Ephesians 2:8–9, 1 Corinthians 15:34, 1 John 1:9, 1 John 5:1, 1 John 5:12–13

If you make a commitment to Christ today, please let me know so I can personally pray for you. Email me at Cherie@CherieJobe.com

Adapted from Joyce Meyers Ministry

GOD'S SURVIVAL TIPS

ACCEPTANCE

"Come to Me, all who are weary and heavy-laden, and I will give you rest." Matthew 11:28

Therefore, there is now no condemnation for those who are in Christ Jesus. Romans 8:1

Wherefore, accept one another, just as Christ also accepted us to the glory of God. Romans 15:7

ADDICTION

You are from God, little children, and have overcome them; because greater is He who is in you than He who is in the world. 1 John 4:4

I can do all things through Christ who strengthens me. Philippians 4:13

Submit therefore to God. Resist the devil and he will flee from you. James 4:7

Anger

Cease from anger and forsake wrath; do not fret; it leads only to evildoing. Psalm 37:8

He who is slow to anger has great understanding. But he who is quick-tempered exalts folly. Proverbs 14:29

Do not be eager in your heart to be angry. For anger resides in the bosom of fools. Ecclesiastes 7:9

Business

"Seek first His kingdom and His righteousness and all these things will be added to you." Matthew 6:33

Commit your works to the Lord, and your plans will be established. Proverbs 16:3

Trust in the Lord with all your heart and do not lean on your own understanding. In all your ways acknowledge Him, and He will make your paths straight. Do not be wise in your own eyes: fear the Lord and turn away from evil. It will be healing to your body and refreshment to your bones. Honor the Lord from your wealth and from the first of all your produce; so your barns will be filled with plenty and your vats will overflow with new wine. Proverbs 3:5–10

Contentment

For He has satisfied the thirsty soul and the hungry soul He has filled with what is good. Psalm 107:9

If we have food and covering, with these we shall be content. 1 Timothy 6:8

Make sure that your character is free from the love of money, being content with what you have; for He Himself has said, "I will never desert you, nor will I forsake you." Hebrews 13:5

Depression

The righteous cry, and the Lord hears and delivers them out of all their troubles. Psalm 34:17

He heals the brokenhearted and binds up all their wounds. Psalm 147:3

"When you pass through the waters, I will be with you; and through the rivers, they will not overflow you. When you walk through the fire, you will not be scorched, nor will the flame burn you." Isaiah 43:2

Doubt

"Therefore I say to you, all things for which you pray and ask, believe that you have received them, and they will be granted you." Mark 11:22–24

Yet, with respect to the promise of God, He did not waver in unbelief but grew strong in faith giving glory to God, and being fully assured that what God had promised, He was able also to perform. Romans 4:20–21

Faithful is He who calls you, and He also will bring it to pass. 1 Thessalonians 5:24

ENVY

Do not fret because of evildoers, be not envious toward wrongdoers. Psalm 37:1

Do not let your heart envy sinners, but live in the fear of the Lord always. Proverbs 23:17

Love is patient, love is kind and is not jealous; love does not brag and is not arrogant. 1 Corinthians 13:4

FEAR

Do not fear them for the Lord your God is the one fighting for you. Deuteronomy 3:22

The Lord is the one who goes ahead of you; He will be with you. He will not fail you or forsake you. Do not fear or be dismayed. Deuteronomy 31:8

Even though I walk through the valley of the shadow of death, I fear no evil, for You are with me; Your rod and Your staff, they comfort me. Psalm 23:4

FORGIVENESS

"If you forgive others for their transgressions, your heavenly Father will also forgive you. But, if you do not forgive others, then your Father will not forgive your transgressions." Matthew 6:14–15

"Whenever you stand praying, forgive, if you have anything against anyone, so that your Father who is in heaven will also forgive you your transgressions." Mark 11:25

Be kind to one another, tenderhearted, forgiving each other, just as God in Christ also has forgiven you. Ephesians 4:32

GOD'S SURVIVAL TIPS

GRIEF

For the Lord has comforted His people and will have compassion on His afflicted. Isaiah 49:13

Cast all your anxiety on Him, because He cares for you. 1 Peter 5:7

"And He will wipe away every tear from their eyes; and there will no longer be any death; there will no longer be any mourning or crying or pain; the first things have passed away." Revelation 21:4

HOPE

Be strong and let your heart take courage, all you who hope in the Lord. Psalm 31:24

For You are my hope; O Lord God. You are my confidence from my youth! Psalm 71:5

Therefore, prepare your minds for action, keep sober in spirit, fix your hope completely on the race to be brought to you at the revelation of Jesus Christ. 1 Peter 1:13

JOY

"These things I have spoken to you so that My joy may be in you, and that your joy may be made full." John 15:11

Though you have not seen Him, you love Him, and though you do not see Him now, but believe in Him, you greatly rejoice with joy inexpressible and full of glory. 1 Peter 1:8

"Therefore you too have grief now, but I will see you again and your heart will rejoice, and no one will take your joy away from you." John 6:22

Loneliness

God is our refuge and strength, a very present help in trouble. Psalm 46:1

He heals the brokenhearted and binds up their wounds. Psalm 147:3

"Teaching them to deserve all that I command you; and lo, I am with you always, even to the end of the age." Matthew 28:20

Motivation

Whatever you do, do your work heartily, as for the Lord rather than for men. Colossians 3:23

Whatever your hand finds to do, do it with all your might. Ecclesiastes 9:10

"Whatever you ask in My name, that will I do so that the Father may be glorified in the Son. If you ask Me anything in My name, I will do it." John 14:13–14

Peace

The Lord will give strength to His people; the Lord will bless His people with peace. Psalm 29:11

"Peace I leave with you; My peace I give to you; not as the world gives do I give to you. Do not let your heart be troubled, nor let it be fearful." John 14:27

Let the peace of Christ rule in your hearts, to which indeed you were called in one body; and be thankful. Colossians 3:15

GOD'S SURVIVAL TIPS

SINGLENESS

Delight yourself in the Lord and He will give you the desires of your heart. Psalm 37:4

God is our refuge and strength, a very present help in trouble. Psalm 46:1

But I want you to be free from concern. One who is unmarried is concerned about the things of the Lord. But one who is married is concerned about the things of the world, how he may please his wife, and his interests are divided... This I say for your own benefit, not to put a restraint upon you, but to promote what is seemly and to secure undistracted devotion to the Lord. 1 Corinthians 7:32-35

SUFFERING

For you have been called for this purpose, since Christ also suffered for you, leaving you an example for you to follow in His steps. 1 Peter 2:21

But if anyone suffers as a Christian, he is not to be ashamed, but is to glorify God in this name! 1 Peter 4:16

God is our refuge and strength, a very present help in trouble. Psalm 46:1

SPIRITUAL GROWTH

Like newborn babies, long for the pure milk of the word, so that by it you may grow in respect to salvation, if you have tasted the kindness of the Lord. 1 Peter 2:2-3

As a result, we are no longer to be children, tossed here and there by waves and carried about by every wind of doctrine, by the trickery of men, by craftiness in deceitful scheming; but speaking the truth in love, we are to grow up in all aspects into Him who is the head, even Christ. Ephesians 4:14–15

Let the word of Christ richly dwell within you, with all wisdom teaching and admonishing one another with psalms and hymns and spiritual songs, singing with the thankfulness in your hearts to God. Colossians 3:16

WAITING

My soul, wait in silence for God only, for my hope is from Him. He only is my rock and my salvation, my stronghold; I shall not be shaken. Psalm 62:5–6

Those who wait for the Lord will gain new strength; they will mount up with wings like eagles, they will run and not get tired, they will walk and not become weary. Isaiah 40:31

Let us hold fast the confession of our hope without wavering, for He who promised is faithful. Hebrews 10:23

WORRY

And my God will supply all your needs according to His riches in glory in Christ Jesus. Philippians 4:19

Casting all your anxiety on Him, because He cares for you. 1 Peter 5:7

"For this reason I say to you, do not be worried about your life, as to what you will eat or what you will drink; nor for your body, as to what you will put on. Is not life more than food and the body more than clothing? Look at the birds in the air, that they do not sow, nor reap, nor gather in barns, and yet your heavenly Father feeds them. Are you not worth much more than they? And who of you by being worried can add a single hour to his life? And why are you worried about clothing? Observe how the lilies of the field grow, they do not toil nor do they spin, yet I say to you that even Solomon in all his glory clothed himself like one of these. But if God so clothes the grass of the field, which is alive today and tomorrow is thrown into the furnace, will He not much more clothe you? You of little faith! Do not worry then, saying 'What will we eat' or 'What will we drink?' or 'What will we wear for clothing? For the Gentiles eagerly seek all these things; for your heavenly Father knows that you need all these things. But seek first His kingdom and His righteousness, and all these things will be added to you. So do not worry about tomorrow; for tomorrow will care for itself. Each day has enough trouble of its own." Matthew 6:25–34

ABOUT THE AUTHOR

Cherie Jobe's call to this ministry was a gradual process that began after her salvation experience on September 14, 1997. She had just turned forty years old and had gone through her second divorce. She had attended church all her life, but she never had accepted Jesus Christ. She had heard of this man all her life, but this day He became more than words on the page of history–He became her Savior. He changed her heart and opened her eyes to the truth that comes from His word. After that day, she felt she was given a second chance at life.

Cherie had tried everything to fill the emptiness and loneliness in the depths of her soul. She believes the Lord used and continues to use her mistakes as examples of how He can change a life.

He has taken her messes and made a message about His love and forgiveness. She believes and teaches that regardless of a person's background or personal mistakes, God has a plan for their life. Isaiah 43:18-19 says, "Do not cling to events of the past or dwell on what happened long ago. Watch for the new thing I am going to do. It is happening already–you can see it now! I will make a road through the wilderness and give you streams of water there."

Cherie surrendered to God's call and follows wherever He leads. It is amazing how He continues to open doors for her to write, to speak, and to connect with kindred spirits at events and conferences for women. She is working and waiting, talking and listening, and always seeking God's direction. Whatever doors God opens, she's walking through.

In her spare time, you might find Cherie camping in God's natural beauty with her amazing husband Jim and their dog Harley. The rest of her time is spent in the kitchen cooking for their four children, two hungry sons-in-law, two daughters-in-law, and four fabulous grandchildren.

This sometimes worn-out hairdresser still loves to tell about bad hair days she has learned from behind her chair–life stories that help women and men to be content, peaceful and strong, even during the bad hair days of life.

Share with Us

Everyone has bad hair days in life. If you have a story you'd like to share, please submit your life story by email to CherieJobe@comcast.net or by mail to Cherie Jobe, P.O. Box 331415, Murfreesboro, TN 37133.

OTHER BOOKS BY CHERIE JOBE

Secrets from Behind the Chair
Publication Date: September 17, 2010
Publisher: Designed by Him Ministry
ISBN: 978-0-615-39718-4

Through a series of heartrending secrets, Cherie Jobe offers the gifts of hope and wisdom, teaching how to be content, peaceful, and strong, even during the bad hair days of life. Her 30 years behind her hairstylists chair have given Cherie volumes to share.

Having learned the "hard knocks way," Cherie offers friendship, candid humor and wise counsel when clients reveal childhood tragedies, relationship troubles, and deeply hidden hurts. In shared stories of secrets no longer feared, these ordinary people find extraordinary strength in hope, love and forgiveness.

Not got a book yet? Go to www.CherieJobe.com.

Cherie Jobe hosts a women's conference every February. More than 300 women attended in 2014. For more information about this event, go to www.CherieJobe.com.

1